Documentation of Associated and Unassociated Caddo Funerary Objects

in the
Stephen F. Austin State University Collections
Nacogdoches, Texas

Timothy K. Perttula, Mark Walters,
Bo Nelson, and Robert Cast

with a contribution by
Robert G. Franciscus

Caddo Nation of Oklahoma • Historic Preservation Program
Binger, Oklahoma

Documentation of Associated and Unassociated
Caddo Funerary Objects
in the Stephen F. Austin State University Collections
Nacogdoches, Texas

Stephen F. Austin State University Press
2010

Second Printing
2015

Library of Congress

Cataloging-in-publication data

Perttula, Timothy K. Walters, Mark. Nelson, Bo. Cast, Robert.
  Documentation of Associated and Unassociated Caddo Funerary Objects in the Stephen F. Austin State University Collections Nacogdoches, Texas / preface by Robert Cast, Tribal Historic Preservation Officer Caddo Nation.
—1st ed.

p.   cm.

COPYRIGHT © 2010
Cover and Text design: George Avery,
Cultural Heritage Research Coordinator

ISBN 978-1-936205-02-8
1. Caddo Indians. 2. Texas—Indians.
3. Texas—Archeology. 3. Texas—Native American Graves.
4. East Texas—Caddo Burial Sites.
5. East Texas—Nacogdoches. I. Perttula, Timothy K.
II. Walters, Mark. III. Nelson, Bo. IV. Cast, Robert

STEPHEN F. AUSTIN STATE UNIVERSITY PRESS
http://sfapress.sfasu.edu
sfapress@sfasu.edu

TABLE OF CONTENTS

List of Figures ....iii-vii

List of Tables viii

Preface ....xi-xii

Acknowledgements xiii

Special Thanks xiv

CHAPTER 1 Introduction and Purpose of the Study..1

    NAGPRA Collections 2
    Documentation of the Ceramic Vessels......................................2

CHAPTER 2 Sites in the NAGPRA Collections..5

    Washington Square Mound (41NA49) 5
        Burial Features in the Reavely-House Mound (Mound 4) 10
        Vessels 11
        Clay Pigments 30
        Organic Remains...31
        Marine Shell Beads 31
        Marine Shell Pendant Fragment and Shell Disc Fragment 36
        Deer Teeth..36
        Lithic Artifact Cache 36
    41NA113 38
    41PN48 39
    41TT135 40
    41SY83 40
    Greasy Creek 41
    Unknown East Texas Caddo Burial Sites 41

CHAPTER 3 Native American Graves Protection and Repatriation
                Act (NAGPRA) Findings and Recommendations....................43

Documentation of Associated and Unassociated Caddo Funerary Objects

References Cited 45

APPENDIX 1   Vessel Recordation Forms, Washington Square Mound Site (41NA49) NAGPRA Collections 51

APPENDIX 2   Preliminary Report on the Skeletal Analysis of Burials from the Washington Square Mound Site (41NA49) in Nacogdoches County, Texas, by *Robert G. Franciscus* 151

APPENDIX 3   Vessel Recordation Forms for NAGPRA Collections from an Unknown East Texas Site or Sites and a Site at Greasy Creek in Camp County, Texas 165

APPENDIX 4   Vessel Recordation Forms for NAGPRA Collections from 41NA113 177

APPENDIX 5   Vessel Recordation Forms for NAGPRA Collections from 41PN48 183

APPENDIX 6   Vessel Recordation Forms for NAGPRA Collections from 41TT135 193

APPENDIX 7   Arrow Points from the Oak Grove Cemetery 197

APPENDIX 8   Vessel Recordation Forms for NAGPRA Collections from 41SY83 201

List of Authors 209

LIST OF FIGURES

Figure 1. Topographic map of the area around the Washington Square Mound site between Banita and La Nana creeks in Nacogdoches County, Texas. From Corbin and Hart (1998: Figure 3), reproduced with the permission of the Texas Archeological Society 1

Figure 2. Portion of the 1900 Sanborn Insurance Map of Nacogdoches showing the locations of historic buildings on the Washington Square Mound site and Mounds 1/2, 3, and 4, based on historic descriptions. NU=Nacogdoches University. Figure reproduced from Corbin and Hart (1998: Figure 4) courtesy of the Texas Archeological Society 6

Figure 3. Views of the Reavely-House Mound: a, looking east at the mound; b, looking southeast at the mound; c, looking northeast at the mound; d, Texas Historical Commission marker on the mound 7-8

Figure 4. Excavations by SFA at the Reavely-House Mound, reproduced from Corbin and Hart (1998: Figure 26), courtesy of the Texas Archeological Society 9

Figure 5. Plan of the Feature 31 burial pit at the Washington Square Mound site, reproduced from Corbin and Hart (1998: Figure 29), courtesy of the Texas Archeological Society 10

Figure 6. Plan of the Feature 95 burial at the Washington Square Mound site, reproduced from Corbin and Hart (1998: Figure 30), with recent modifications adding vessel numbers to the figure, courtesy of the Texas Archeological Society 12

Figure 7. Selected vessels from Feature 31: a, F31-1; b, F31-2; c, F31-3; d, F31-5; e, F31-9; f, F31-10; g, F31-12; h, F31-14 16-17

Figure 8. Selected vessels from Feature 95: a, F95-4; b, F95-8; c, F95-11; d, F95-13; e, F95-14; f, F95-19; g, F95-20; h, F95-21; i, F95-23; j, F95-27; k, F95-28; l, F95-33 17-19

Figure 9. Other vessels from the Washington Square Mound site: a, from the Oak Grove cemetery, found in 1957; b, brushed-punctated vessel reconstructed from parts of two or three vessels, found in 1939 on the grounds of the T. J. Rusk Middle School 23

Figure 10. Red clay pigment from Feature 95, Vessel 13 31

Documentation of Associated and Unassociated Caddo Funerary Objects

Figure 11. Marine shell columella beads from the wrist area of Feature 31: a, lot 283; b, F31-B, film canister 1; c, film canister 6, Cabinet 25............32-33

Figure 12. Marine shell columella beads from Feature 95: a, left wrist; b, right wrist..35

Figure 13. Marine shell pendant fragment from Feature 95 36

Figure 14. Lithic artifact cache from Feature 31..37

Figure 15. *Olivella* marine shell bead from 41NA113, Burial 1......................................39

Figure 16. Incised-punctated utility ware vessel from the Washington Square Mound site, found at the Oak Grove Cemetery..53

Figure 17. Brushed-punctated utility ware vessel found on the grounds of the T. J. Rusk Middle School on the Washington Square Mound site...................55

Figure 18. Nacogdoches Engraved compound bowl, F31-1 57

Figure 19. Nacogdoches Engraved bottle, F31-2...59

Figure 20. Nacogdoches Engraved compound bowl, F31-3 61

Figure 21. Plain bowl, F31-4 63

Figure 22. Washington Square Paneled compound bowl, F31-5 65

Figure 23. Brushed-incised-punctated utility ware vessel, F31-6 67

Figure 24. Reavely Brushed-Incised jar vessel section, F31-7...69

Figure 25. Reavely Brushed-Incised jar, F31-8 71

Figure 26. Nacogdoches Engraved bottle, F31-9...73

Figure 27. Reavely Brushed-Incised jar, F31-10 75

Figure 28. Brushed-punctated carinated bowl, F31-11 77

Figure 29. Plain olla, F31-12 79

Figure 30. Plain jar, F31-13 81

Figure 31. Punctated jar, F31-14 83

Figure 32. Incised effigy vessel from Feature 31, Vessel F31-15 85

Figure 33. Nacogdoches Engraved carinated bowl, F95-1 87

Figure 34. Punctated vessel fragment from Feature 95, F95-2: a, rim sherds;
b, body and base sherds 89

Figure 35. Undetermined engraved carinated bowl, F95-3 91

Figure 36. Reavely Brushed-Incised jar, F95-4 93

Figure 37. Vessel F95-6: a, side view; b, view looking down at Redwine
mode rim 95

Figure 38. Nacogdoches Engraved carinated bowl, F95-7 97

Figure 39. Nacogdoches Engraved compound bowl, F95-8 99

Figure 40. Brushed-punctated jar, F95-9 101

Figure 41. Nacogdoches Engraved bowl, F95-10 103

Figure 42. Incised-punctated carinated bowl, F95-11 105

Figure 43. Undetermined engraved compound bowl, F95-12 107

Figure 44. Washington Square Paneled jar, F95-13 109

Figure 45. Undetermined engraved compound bowl, F95-14 111

Figure 46. Engraved-rocker stamped vessel from Feature 95, F95-15 113

Figure 47. Nacogdoches Engraved compound bowl, F95-16 115

Figure 48. Undetermined engraved compound bowl, F95-17 117

Figure 49. Nacogdoches Engraved bowl, F95-18 119

Figure 50. Undetermined engraved carinated bowl, F95-19 121

Figure 51. Reavely Brushed-Incised jar, F95-20 123

Documentation of Associated and Unassociated Caddo Funerary Objects

Figure 52. Washington Square Paneled carinated bowl: a, side view; b, view of scalloped lip 125

Figure 53. Undetermined engraved carinated bowl, F95-22: a, side view; b, view of Redwine mode rim 127

Figure 54. Nacogdoches Engraved bottle, F95-23 129

Figure 55. Nacogdoches Engraved bowl, F95-25 131

Figure 56. Plain carinated bowl, F95-26 133

Figure 57. Nacogdoches Engraved bottle, F95-27 135

Figure 58. Undetermined incised-punctated jar, F95-28 137

Figure 59. Washington Square Paneled carinated bowl, F95-29 139

Figure 60. Plain carinated bowl, F95-30 141

Figure 61. Plain carinated bowl, F95-31 143

Figure 62. Nacogdoches Engraved carinated bowl, F95-32: a, side view; b, view of Redwine mode rim 145

Figure 63. Nacogdoches Engraved, nee Nacogdoches Punctated carinated bowl, F95-33 147

Figure 64. Nacogdoches Engraved compound bowl, F95-34 149

Figure 65. Vessel 31.1, a plain bottle, from an undetermined Caddo burial site 167

Figure 66. Engraved compound bowl from unknown site, Vessel 31.2 169

Figure 67. Undetermined engraved carinated bowl from an unknown site in Cherokee County, Texas, Vessel 31.3 171

Figure 68. Ripley Engraved bowl from the Greasy Creek area, Camp County, Texas 173

Figure 69. Undetermined plain carinated bowl from the Greasy Creek area, Camp County, Texas 175

Figure 70. Engraved bowl from 41NA113 179

Figure 71. Patton Engraved bowl from 41NA113 181

Figure 72. Brushed bottle from 41PN48 185

Figure 73. Plain carinated bowl, PN48-2, from 41PN48 187

Figure 74. Brushed jar from 41PN48 189

Figure 75. Plain bowl from 41PN48, PN48-4 191

Figure 76. Plain bowl from 41TT135 195

Figure 77. Perdiz arrow points from the vessel found at the Oak Grove cemetery 199

Figure 78. Engraved bottle from 41SY83, a. side view, b. top view 203

Figure 79. Plain bowl from 41SY83 205

Figure 80. Plain handled bowl or ladle from 41SY83, top and side views 207

Documentation of Associated and Unassociated Caddo Funerary Objects

LIST OF TABLES

Table 1 Vessels from the Washington Square Mound site (41NA49) 13-15

Table 2 Vessel volume (in liters) comparisons by feature 25

Table 3 Temper classes in the Feature 31 and 95 vessels 26

Table 4 Decorated fine wares and utility wares in funerary vessels and non-mortuary vessel sherds from the Washington Square Mound site 27

Table 5 Firing conditions observed in the Feature 31 and 95 vessels 28

Table 6 Marine shell beads from Feature 31 32

Table 7 Marine shell beads from Feature 95 34

Table 8 Lithic artifact cache in Feature 31 at the Washington Square Mound site 37

PREFACE

In May of 2006, the anthropology program for Stephen F. Austin State University (SFA) and its archeological repository were in danger of closing. Frantic emails and list server commentaries were bouncing back and forth between other universities, state agencies, and Texas archeologists regarding the inevitable closing and what needed to be done to keep the doors open. A few of the more focused discussions revolved around the question of what the university would now do with all of the state held in trust collections that the late Dr. James E. Corbin had brought to the university over his many years as a professor and archeologist at the SFA. A number of Dr. Corbin's past graduate students voiced concerns over the closing of the program and its impact to the legacy Dr. Corbin left behind. Many of the artifacts in the collections had been excavated under Antiquities Permits issued by the Texas Historical Commission, who also voiced their concern with the university. The Texas Archeological Society (TAS) had done field work in Nacogdoches in 1985 and the university still held these collections. There were also a number of collections in the repository that fell under the purview of the Native American Graves Protection and Repatriation Act (NAGPRA) of 1990.

Dr. Corbin had first initiated consultation with the Caddo Nation regarding the NAGPRA collections through correspondence dated November 29, 1993. The letter explained that most of the collections came from the Washington Square Mound Site and that these were from excavations that took place during the summers of 1979, 1980, and 1981. He further explained that "[n]o report of the excavations has been published to date."

By June of 2006, the Caddo Nation had written letters and made a number of phone calls to the university. Meetings were scheduled. The university was clearly out of compliance with NAGPRA. What this really meant in the scheme of things (as we explained during the initial meeting) was that ALL of the federal funding that the university received could be put in jeopardy until they complied with the NAGPRA.

As a result of the first meeting, on September 7, 2006, it was agreed that the SFA would hire a Doctorate level archeologist part-time to come in and begin accessing the collections and the condition of the repository. By October of 2006, the university had hired Dr. George Avery for this job.

Another task we proposed during our meetings with the university was that SFA contract the NAGPRA related work (preparing inventories and findings for the National Park Service) to our Historic Preservation Program. We provided them copies of some of our past reports and it was agreed that this work could be done under a contract that would be agreed upon by both SFA and the Caddo Nation. This is when our real work began.

Over what now seems like an eternity, an electronic contract bounced back and forth between the newly appointed Chairperson of the Sociology Department, Dr. Jerry Williams and me, the contract being revised only as each party would decide to smaller compromises. Suddenly we came to standstill. The university maintained that the contract as a standard state contract only state law applied to how it could be written, developed, and executed. However, the Caddo Nation would not under the circumstances waive any of its Sovereign immunity as a federally recognized tribal government and disregarded that any breach of contract would or could be addressed by state laws.

Thanks to Dr. Williams and his persistency to make sure that the university continued in its good faith effort to comply with NAGPRA, he (working along with the university's Office of the General Counsel) averted what could have easily been a disastrous beginning in our working relationship with SFA to finally address the tribe's NAGPRA collections housed there. The contract was eventually signed and the work accomplished under that contract is the report you now hold in your hands.

These pages represent over two years of phone calls, emails, letters, meetings, discussions, arguments, and ultimately, a gratifying partnership among archeologists, a university, and a federally recognized tribal government. To date, the program at SFA is still going strong, with Dr. Avery and Dr. Leslie Cecil now working full-time for the anthropology program. With these NAGPRA inventories completed, the repository updated, and a full accounting of the artifacts in the SFA repository current, I know Jim Corbin would be smiling, happy about it all.

Robert Cast
Tribal Historic Preservation Officer
Caddo Nation
September 16, 2008

ACKNOWLEDGMENTS

We would like to thank the following people for helping us with this project. First, Drs. Jerry Williams, George Avery, and Leslie Cecil at SFA greatly facilitated the work, especially Dr. Williams in getting a contract prepared and signed, and they went out of their way to make sure the documentation effort went smoothly.

Some figures in this report had been previously prepared by James E. Corbin and John P. Hart for a 1998 article on the Washington Square Mound site, and these are reproduced here with the permission of the Texas Archeological Society. Sandy Hannum prepared one of the final versions of the Washington Square Mound site burial plans used in this report, and Bo Nelson took the many artifact photographs.

SPECIAL THANKS

We would like to take this opportunity to acknowledge the pivotal role played by Bobby Gonzalez, NAGPRA Coordinator for the Caddo Nation of Oklahoma, in the development of this volume. Bobby had a cordial relationship with Jim Corbin, and while SFA was not in total compliance with the letter of the law, certainly SFA was in compliance with the spirit of NAGPRA through Jim Corbin's open communication with Bobby Gonzalez and the Caddo Nation. With Jim Corbin's passing, the personal link between the Caddo Nation and SFA was interrupted, but it was Bobby Gonzalez who made sure that this link was renewed. Bobby's efforts resulted in SFA hiring a consultant to assist with NAGPRA compliance and also funding the documentation and publishing of the NAGPRA collections at SFA. There are not many NAGPRA documentation projects that have been conducted and published by the tribe with funds provided by the parent institution. This all came about through the inspiration of Bobby Gonzalez, and we at SFA are grateful for his vision, diplomacy, and friendship over the last few years.

Jerry Williams
Chair, Department of Social and Cultural Analysis
Stephen F. Austin State University

George Avery
Cultural Heritage Resource Coordinator
Stephen F. Austin State University

Chapter 1

INTRODUCTION AND PURPOSE OF THE STUDY

This report concerns the documentation of Native American Graves Protection and Repatriation Act (NAGPRA) funerary objects from prehistoric sites in the collections at Stephen F. Austin State University (SFA) in Nacogdoches, Texas. The purpose of this documentation is to determine the cultural affiliation of these NAGPRA funerary objects so that SFA can meet their legal responsibilities under the NAGPRA. A secondary purpose is to review the character of the funerary assemblage—especially the distinctive ceramic vessel found in two burials in the Reavely Mound—at the Washington Square Mound site (see Hart 1982; Corbin and Hart 1998), in the city of Nacogdoches (Figure 1), in light of the history of the ancestral Caddo occupation of this important mound center.

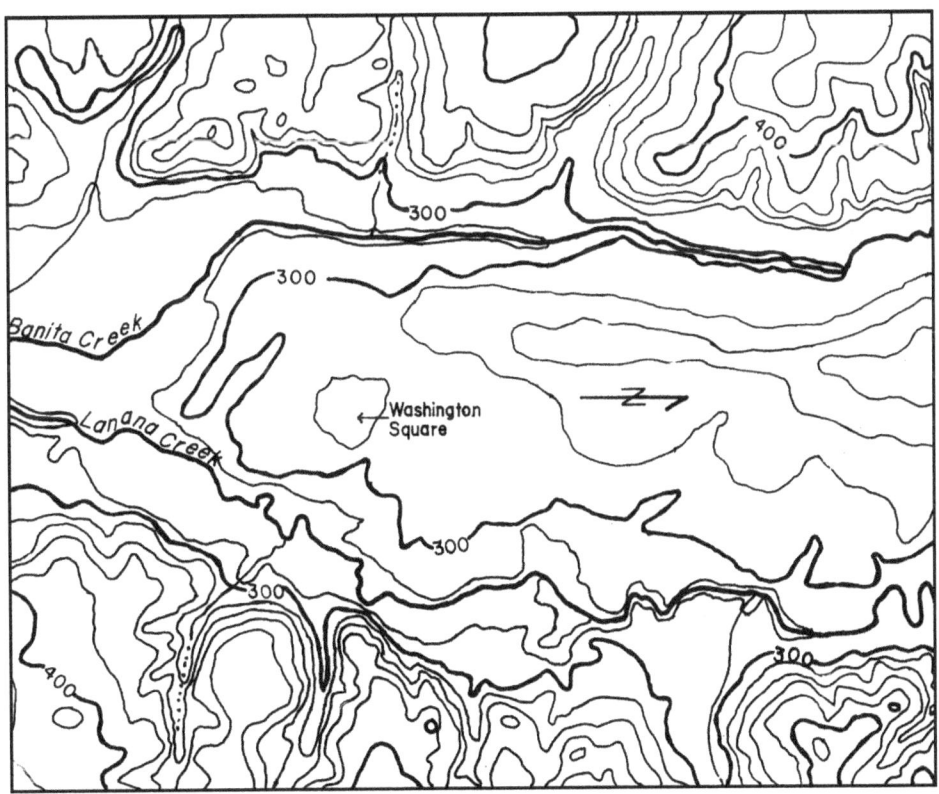

Figure 1. Topographic map of the area around the Washington Square Mound site between Banita and La Nana creeks in Nacogdoches County, Texas. From Corbin and Hart (1998: Figure 3), reproduced with the permission of the Texas Archeological Society.

DOCUMENTATION OF ASSOCIATED AND UNASSOCIATED CADDO FUNERARY OBJECTS

NAGPRA COLLECTIONS

The SFA NAGPRA collection of funerary objects are from five known and recorded prehistoric sites in northeastern and East Texas. Most of the NAGPRA funerary objects are whole ceramic vessels (n=49) from the Washington Square Mound site (41NA49), with smaller numbers from 41NA113 (n=2), 41PN48 (n=4), 41TT135 (n=1), 41SY83 (n=3), two from the Greasy Creek area of Camp County, Texas (see Perttula and Nelson 2004), two from unknown sites in East Texas, and a final vessel from an unknown burial site in Cherokee County, Texas. Other funerary offerings in the SFA NAGPRA collection of funerary objects include marine shell beads, a marine shell pendant fragment, a marine shell disc fragment, deer teeth, clay pigments, charred organic debris, and a cache of lithic debris, one core, and one flake tool. Each of these different kinds of funerary objects are discussed in the context of the archeological findings from the sites listed above, where that information is available.

There are human remains in the SFA collections from the Washington Square Mound site. These remains were not documented during this project, as they have been previously studied by Robert G. Franciscus (1985). His report is included as Appendix 2 of this final report.

DOCUMENTATION OF THE CERAMIC VESSELS

Because of the number of ceramic vessels in the SFA NAGPRA collections, we established a documentation protocol to assist in the study of each of the vessels. Each of the ceramic vessels in the collections is described and illustrated utilizing a consistent set of ceramic morphological, functional, and stylistic attributes modeled after the presentations in Cast et al. (2006); Gadus and Fields (1996); Gonzalez et al. (2005), Perttula et al. (1998, 2008), and Perttula (2005, ed.). The purpose of the documentation is to thoroughly characterize the assemblage of ceramic vessels in the collections. Appendix 1, 3-8 are the completed vessel recordation forms from the Washington Square Mound site, 41NA113, 41PN48, 41TT135, 41SY83, and several whole vessels from less certain and undocumented site contexts (including at least one vessel from Cherokee County, Texas, and two from the Greasy Creek area of Camp County, Texas).

Vessel illustrations include a photograph of each vessel. Hart (1982) also provides scaled drawings of the motifs on many of the Washington Square Mound vessels.

The following attributes were employed in this ceramic vessel study:

Non-plastics: Deliberate and indeterminate materials in the paste (Rice 1987:411), including a variety of tempers (grog or crushed sherds, bone, hematite, shell, quartz sands, etc.) and "particulate matter of some size." The grog, bone, and hematite non-plastics appear to have been deliberately added to the paste as tempers. The bone used for temper had been burned and calcined, then crushed, before it was added to the paste.

Vessel Form: Vessel form categories include open containers (bowls, carinated bowls, and compound bowls) and restricted containers, including jars and bottles. As restricted containers, jars allow access by hand, but bottles do not (Brown 1996:335). Other form attributes that were recorded include the rim profile (outflaring or everted, vertical or standing, and inverted), lip profile (rolled to the exterior, rounded, flat, or thinned), and base shape (flat or rounded).

Core Colors: Observations on ceramic cross-section colors permit consideration of oxidation patterns (Teltser 1993:Figure 2A-H), and thus the conditions under which the vessel was fired and then cooled after firing. Comments are included for these attributes on the presence and location of fire-clouding, sooting or smudging from cooking use (Skibo 1992), and charred organic remains.

Wall Thickness: Thickness was recorded in millimeters, using a vernier caliper, at the lip, along the rim, at several points along the body, and at the base when possible (only for the vessels that were not complete).

Interior and Exterior Surface Treatment: The primary methods of finishing the surface of the vessel include smoothing, burnishing, and polishing (Rice 1987:138). Brushing is a popular method of roughening the surface (particularly the body) of large and small Middle (ca. A.D. 1200-1400) and Late Caddo (ca. A.D. 1400-1680) period cooking jars, but is here considered a decorative treatment rather than solely a functional surface treatment (cf. Rice 1987:138), although not all Caddo ceramic analysts treat brushing as a decorative treatment (cf. Gadus et al. 2006:31). Smoothing creates "a finer and more regular surface...[and] has a matte rather than a lustrous finish" (Rice 1987:138). Burnishing, on the other hand, creates an irregular lustrous finish marked by parallel facets left by the burnishing tool (perhaps a pebble or bone). A polished surface treatment is marked by a uniform and highly lustrous surface finish, done when the vessel is dry, but without "the pronounced parallel facets produced by burnishing leather-hard clay" (Rice 1987:138).

The application of a hematite-rich clay slip (Ferring and Perttula 1987), either red or black after firing in an oxidizing or reducing (i.e., low-oxygen) environment, is another form of surface treatment noted in this assemblage. The clay slip is more frequently applied on the vessel exterior than on the interior surface, and then was either burnished or polished after it was leather-hard or dry.

Height and Orifice Diameter: These attributes, measured in centimeters, were recorded with a ruler.

Diameter at Bottom of Rim and Base Diameter: Also recorded in millimeters using a ruler, these attributes permit characterization of the overall contour and shape of the vessel.

Volume: Vessel volume in liters was determined by filling (to within 1 mm of the lip) the vessel with lentil seeds, then dumping the lentil seeds in containers of known volume. In estimating the volume of vessels with holes, the vessel was first filled with a cloth that conformed to vessel contours, then the lentil seeds were poured into the depression in the cloth to within 1 mm of the top of the lip. Then they were dumped into containers of known volume. In cases where the vessels were not (or could not) be reconstructed, but measurements of height and orifice diameter were be obtained, volumes were estimated by comparison with known vessel volumes of specific forms (i.e., carinated bowl, jar, bottle, compound bowl, and bowl) in other documented Caddo vessel assemblages.

Decoration: Decorative techniques present in the SFA NAGPRA vessel collection from sites in northeastern and East Texas include engraving, incising, punctating, brushing, neck banding, and appliquéing, and on certain vessels, combinations of decorative techniques (i.e., brushed-punctated) created the decorative elements and motifs. Engraving was done with a sharp tool when the vessel was either leather-hard, or after it was fired, while the other decorative techniques were executed with tools (incising and punctation), by adding strips of clay to the wet body (appliqué), by crimping the coils (neck banding), using frayed sticks or grass stems (brushing) dragged across the body surface, or fingernails (certain forms of punctations), when the vessel was wet or still plastic. Excising is considered a form of engraved decoration, where the clay is deliberately and closely marked/scraped and carved away with a sharp tool, usually to create triangular elements (the pendant triangle or small tick marks) or crescent-shaped elements that separate or serve to define scrolls (Suhm and Jelks 1962:Plate 64a, b, f).

Another form of vessel decoration is the use of red (hematite or ochre) or white (kaolin clay) clay pigments that have been smeared or rubbed into the engraved lines of certain vessels.

Type: The kinds of named ceramic types in the SFA NAGPRA collections follow the work of Suhm and Jelks (1962), Corbin and Hart (1998), Hart (1982), and Thurmond (1990).

Chapter 2

SITES IN THE NAGPRA COLLECTIONS

Washington Square Mound (41NA49)

The Washington Square Mound site (41NA49) is an important prehistoric Caddo multiple mound center in East Texas (Corbin and Hart 1998). The site, most of which is on property owned by the Nacogdoches Independent School District, is located on an upland interfluve (310 feet amsl) between Banita Creek on the west and La Nana Creek on the east (see Figure 1).

The site appears to have primarily been occupied by ancestors of the modern-day Caddo Indian peoples between ca. A.D. 1200-1400 (Corbin and Hart 1998: Table 4). During this occupation, the Caddo erected at least three mounds, the University Mound or Mounds 1/2, Mound 3, and Mound 4 or the Reavely-House Mound (Figure 2). Mound 1/2 was constructed by the Caddo over an important building (Corbin and Hart 1998:71), as was apparently also the case for Mound 3, the largest of the known mounds at Washington Square (Corbin and Hart 1998:55).

Mound 4, the Reavely-House Mound (Figure 3a-d), is a Caddo burial mound with at least six known burial pits (Figure 4), based on archeological investigations by SFA in 1979 and 1981. During the course of that work, initially designed "to obtain a stratigraphic profile of the mound" (Corbin and Hart 1998:67), two shaft burial features were identified and excavated in the mound: Feature 31 and Feature 95 (see Figure 4). The bulk of the SFA NAGPRA objects discussed in this report come from these two burial features. Based on the richness and diversity of funerary offerings placed with the Caddo individuals in these two burial features, and their interment in a specially constructed burial or mortuary mound, there is no doubt that the individuals in Features 31 and 95 were amongst the "highest ranking individual(s) in the society" (Story 1990:339) that lived around the Washington Square Mound, and used the mound site for both religious and political ceremonies.

According to Story (1990:339), the prehistoric Caddo shaft burials associated with earthen mounds like those from Washington Square were lavish and expensive (in terms of the exotic funerary offerings placed with the burials and the labor expended to excavate the shaft burial as well as construct the mortuary mound). They also had "the distinction of being placed in a relatively large and deep pit dug into, or capped by, a mound...these burials were embellished by numerous offerings, many of materials indicating the existence of long distance trade networks possibly controlled by elites."

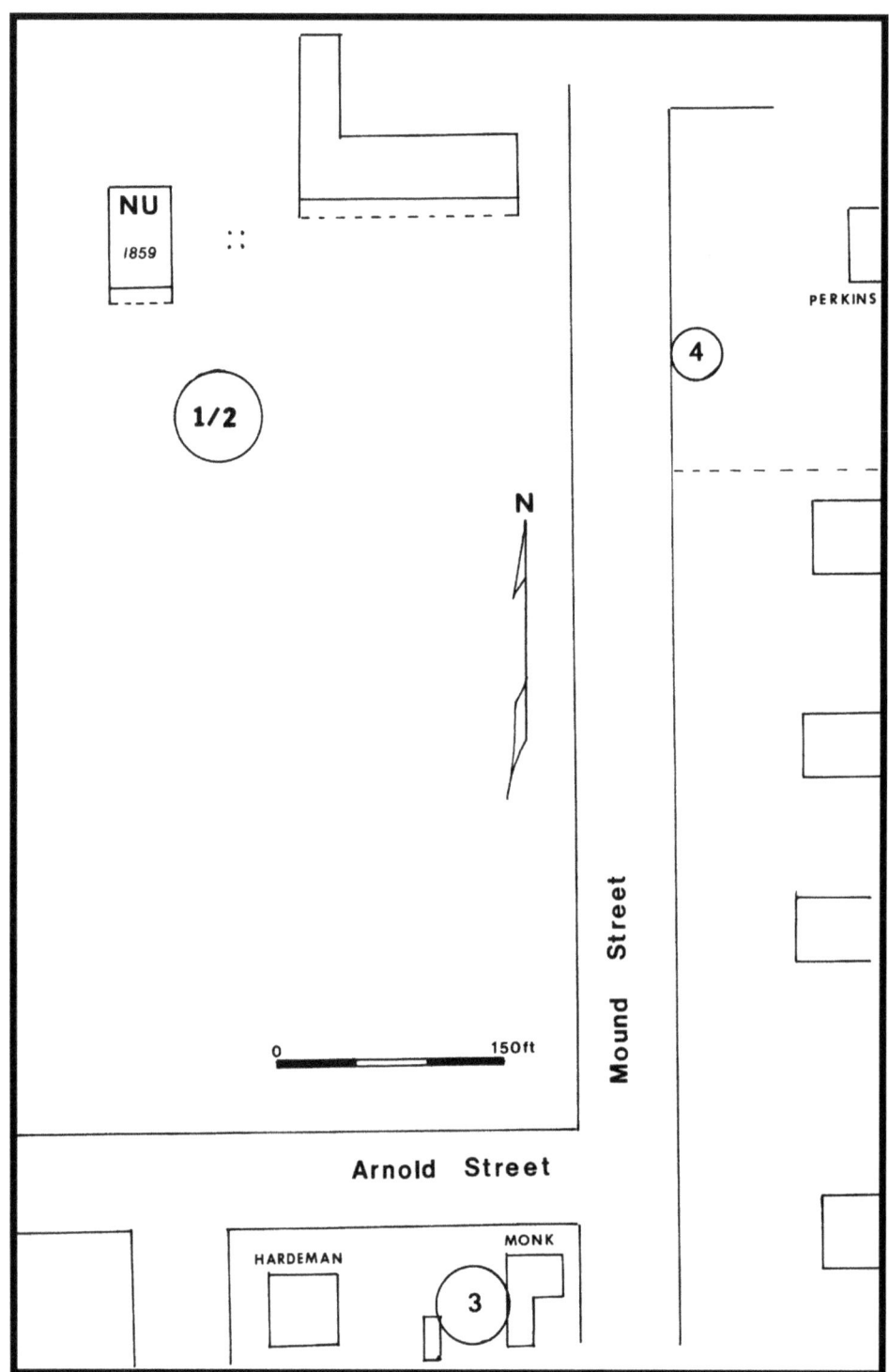

Figure 2. Portion of the 1900 Sanborn Insurance Map of Nacogdoches showing the locations of historic buildings on the Washington Square Mound site and Mounds 1/2, 3, and 4, based on historic descriptions. NU=Nacogdoches University. Figure reproduced from Corbin and Hart (1998: Figure 4) courtesy of the Texas Archeological Society.

Figure 3a. View of the Reavely-House Mound, looking east at the mound.

Figure 3b. View of the Reavely-House Mound, looking southeast at the mound.

Figure 3c. View of the Reavely-House Mound, looking northeast at the mound.

Figure 3d. View of the Reavely-House Mound, Texas Historical Commission marker on the mound.

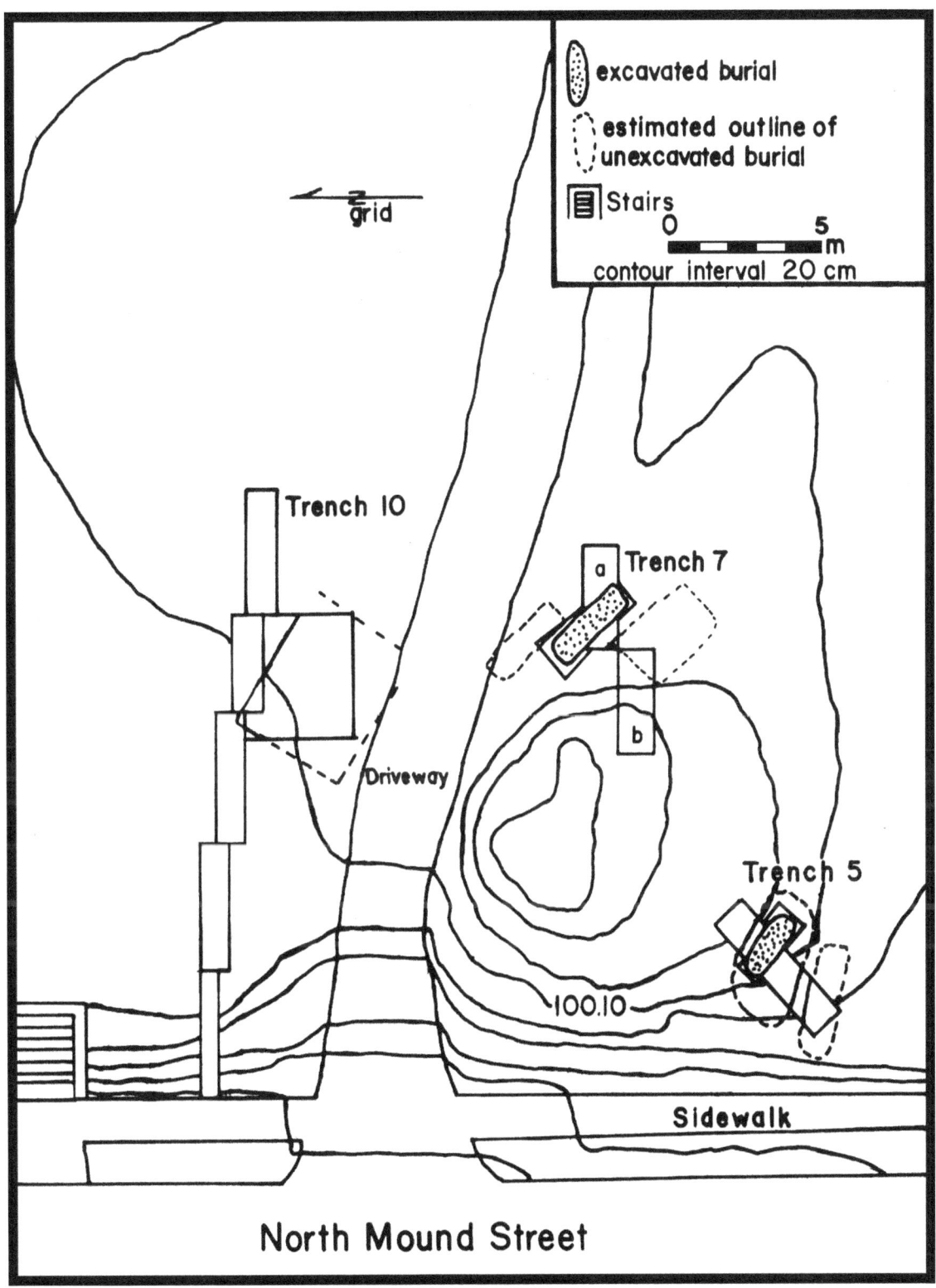

Figure 4. Excavations by SFA at the Reavely-House Mound, reproduced from Corbin and Hart (1998: Figure 26), courtesy of the Texas Archeological Society.

Burial Features in the Reavely-House Mound (Mound 4)

Feature 31 is the burial of an apparently young adult male Caddo individual (see Appendix 2) placed near the southwestern part of the mound. The deceased was placed in a 160 x 105 cm pit, with the head at the southeastern end of the burial (Figure 5). Fifteen ceramic vessels were placed around the edges of the burial feature, along with 13 marine shell columella beads (with some around the wrist area, probably having been worn as a bracelet), and a cache (probably inside a leather bag) of 11 lithic artifacts near what would have been the feet of the deceased.

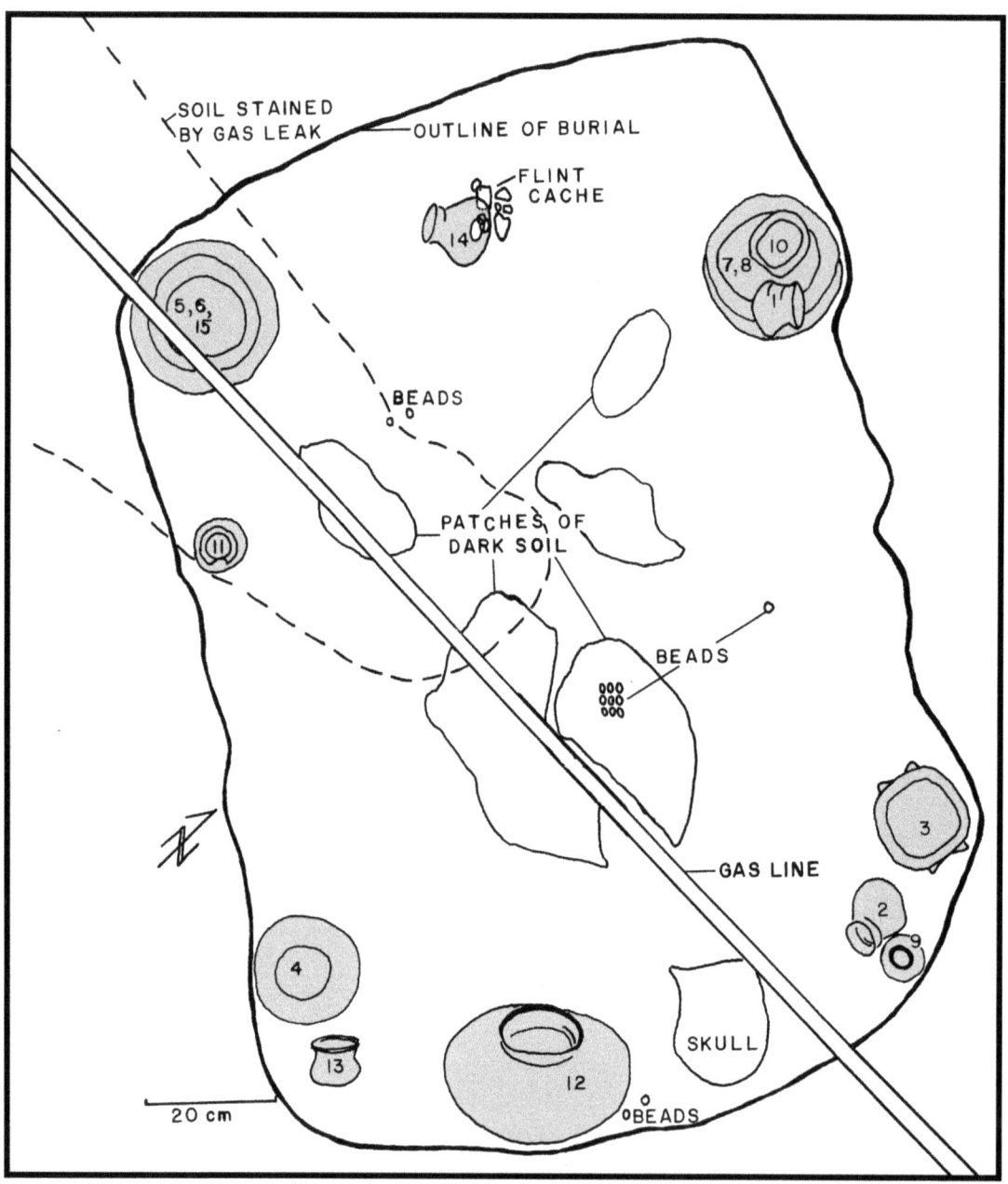

Figure 5. Plan of the Feature 31 burial pit at the Washington Square Mound site, reproduced from Corbin and Hart (1998: Figure 29), courtesy of the Texas Archeological Society.

There were several darkly-stained soil patches in the central part of the burial pit (see Figure 5), and Corbin and Hart (1998:68) suggest that these mark decayed organic materials, probably baskets or matting. They further note a small area of charred wood and fire-reddened earth by Vessel 12, indicating that a small fire had been placed in the burial pit before the vessel was laid down on it. This fire's purpose may have been to burn food offerings placed in the grave during the burial ceremonies (cf. Gonzalez et al. 2005:55-59).

Feature 95 was located along the eastern part of the Reavely-House Mound (see Figure 4), more than 5 m from Feature 31. Two individuals were placed in the burial pit, an adult female on the pit floor (B-II), and a sub-adult male (B-I) laying atop the woman (Figure 6, see also Appendix 2). The burial pit measured 280 x 130 cm in length and width. Both individuals had cranially modeled skulls, a distinctive Caddo cranial treatment (Derrick and Wilson 1997). This burial feature has a northwest-southeast orientation, with the heads of both deceased near the eastern end of the pit.

The floor of the burial pit was encountered at 90 cm bs, where a bright yellow clay strata was encountered, especially near the two bodies; underneath was a red clay C-horizon. The yellow clay may have been obtained from a nearby Weches Formation bedrock outcrop. The remainder of the burial fill was a red (2.5YR 4/6) clay.

The burials and funerary offerings (primarily ceramic vessels) were laid on a 6-8 cm thick organic layer (matting?) placed on this yellow clay. "Organic staining and debris in and around the vessels and skeletal remains suggest that the individuals were both covered with some material distinct from clothing at the time of interment" (Corbin and Hart 1998:69).

Funerary offerings in Feature 95 include 32 vessels[1], pigments of various colors in a number of vessels, marine shell columella beads on the wrists of the adult female, a marine shell pendant from the chest area of the adult female, and a shell disc. A number of vessels had clay pigment placed in them, as well as small amount of the same yellow clay that covered the burial pit floor.

Vessels

The SFA NAGPRA collections from the Washington Square Mound site include 49 vessels, 47 from burial features (Features 31 and 95) and two from uncertain contexts within the site. These vessels occur in a variety of forms, including jars of various sizes (n=14), carinated bowls (n=15) in at least three sizes, compound bowls of two sizes (n=9), small bowls (n=6), large bottles (n=4), two in each burial, and one olla (Table 1). Almost 88% of the vessels are decorated, with more than half of the decorated vessels having engraved designs (Figures 7a-e and 8b, e-f, i-j). Several of these fine ware vessels also had either a white or red clay pigment rubbed in the engraved lines.

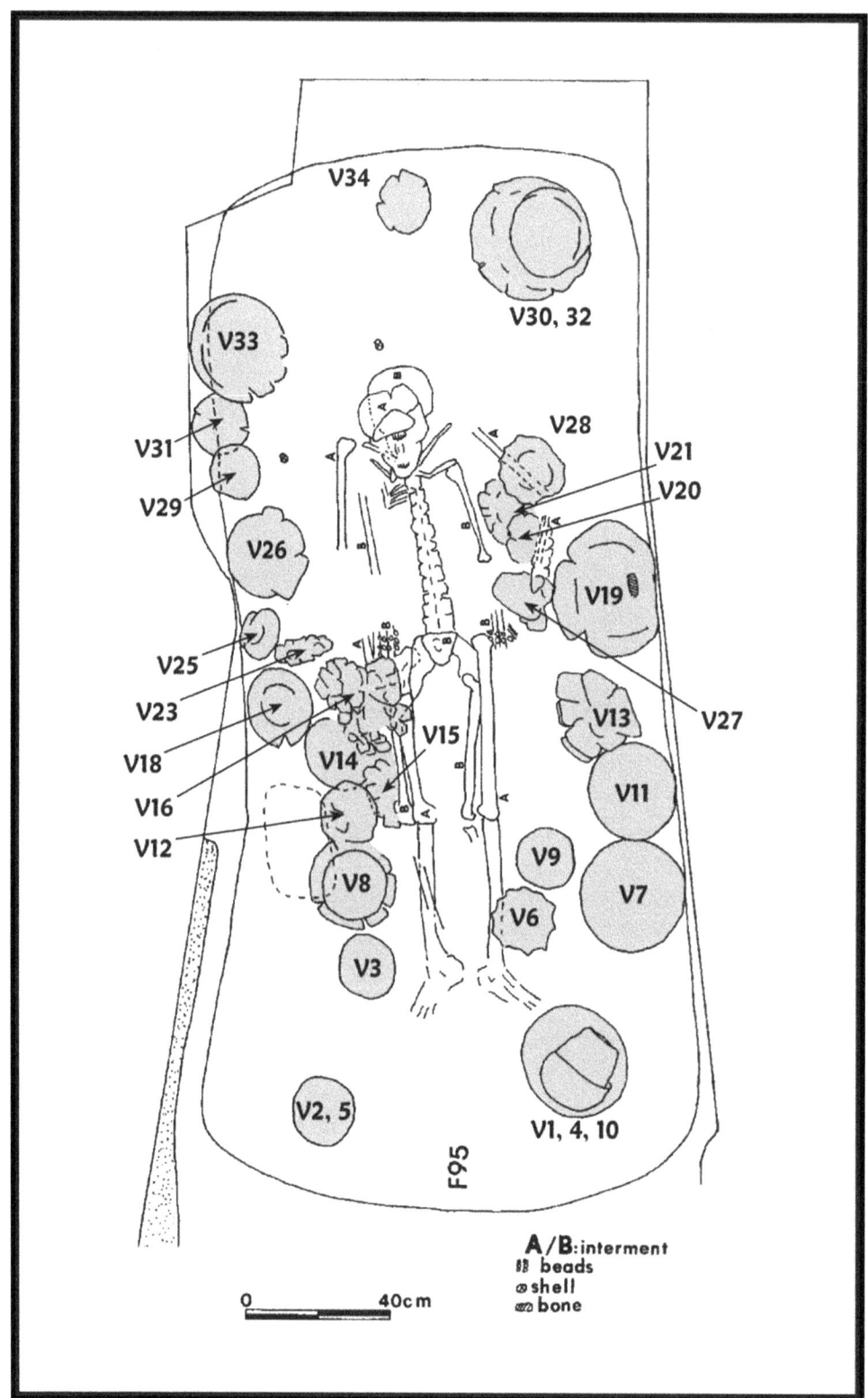

Figure 6. Plan of the Feature 95 burial at the Washington Square Mound site, reproduced from Corbin and Hart (1998: Figure 30), with recent modifications adding vessel numbers to the figure, courtesy of the Texas Archeological Society.

Table 1. Vessels from the Washington Square Mound site (41NA49).

Vessel No.	Temper	Height (cm)	Orifice Diameter (cm)	Volume (liters)	Decoration	Type
<u>Jar</u>						
31.6	grog	17.7	14.5	2.3	incised-punctated	Undetermined
39.1	bone-hematite	34.0	25.5	11.2	brushed-punctated	Undetermined
F31-6	bone-grog	N/A	N/A	N/A	brushed-punctated	Undetermined
F31-7	bone-grog	12.2	18.0	1.9	brushed-punctated-appliqued	Reavely Brushed-Incised
F31-8	grog-hematite	N/A	N/A	N/A	brushed-punctated	Reavely Brushed-Incised
F31-10	grog	10.5	13.1	0.8	brushed-punctated	Reavely Brushed-Incised
F31-13	bone-organics	10.0	11.9	0.7	plain	Undetermined
F31-14	grog	13.6	8.7	0.8	tool punctated	Undetermined
F95-2	grog-hematite	N/A	N/A	N/A	tool punctated	Undetermined
F95-4	grog	15.4	16.5	1.5	brushed-incised-appliqued-punctated	Reavely Brushed-Incised
F95-9	grog	10.2	14.5	0.9	brushed-punctated	Undetermined
F95-13	grog-bone-hematite	13.0	17.0	1.3	incised-punctated	Washington Square Paneled
F95-20	grog	N/A	11.6	N/A	brushed-punctated-appliqued	Reavely Brushed-Incised
F95-28	grog	14.6	12.8	1.1	incised-punctated	Undetermined
<u>Carinated bowl</u>						
F31-11	bone-grog	5.0	7.7	0.15	brushed-punctated	Undetermined
F95-1	bone-hematite-grog	16.8	28.5	4.4	engraved	Nacogdoches Engraved
F95-3	grog	7.5	14.5	0.7	engraved	Undetermined
F95-7	bone	12.0	24.4	1.8	engraved, red pigment	Nacogdoches Engraved
F95-11	grog-hematite	10.5	22.5	1.4	incised-punctated	Undetermined
F95-15	grog-bone-hematite	9.5	15.7	0.9	engraved-rocker stamped	Undetermined
F95-19	grog	11.0	25.5	1.7	engraved	Undetermined

Documentation of Associated and Unassociated Caddo Funerary Objects

Table 1. Vessels from the Washington Square Mound site (41NA49), cont.

Vessel No.	Temper	Height (cm)	Orifice Diameter (cm)	Volume (liters)	Decoration	Type
Carinated bowl, cont.						
F95-21	grog	8.0	19.5	0.9	tool punctated	Washington Square Paneled
F95-22	grog	6.0	15.0	0.55	engraved	Undetermined
F95-26	bone	11.5	17.0	1.2	plain	Undetermined
F95-29	grog-hematite	7.5	14.8	0.7	incised-punctated	Washington Square Paneled
F95-30	grog-bone-hematite	11.0	29.5	1.95	plain	Undetermined
F95-31	bone-grog	7.0	15.5	0.7	plain	Undetermined
F95-32	grog-bone-hematite	7.5	23.5	1.1	engraved	Nacogdoches Engraved
F95-33	grog-bone	13.5	27.0	3.2	punctated	"Nacogdoches Punctated"
Compound bowl						
F31-1	grog	7.5	11.8	0.7	engraved	Nacogdoches Engraved
F31-3	grog-hematite	6.5	16.5	0.9	engraved, white pigment	Nacogdoches Engraved
F31-5	grog	10.6	25.0	2.1	engraved-punctated	Washington Square Paneled
F95-8	grog-hematite	12.5	19.9	2.0	engraved	Nacogdoches Engraved
F95-12	bone-hematite	8.0	16.3	1.0	engraved	Undetermined
F95-14	grog	8.5	18.0	1.2	engraved	Undetermined
F95-16	grog-bone	N/A	N/A	N/A	engraved, white pigment	Nacogdoches Engraved
F95-17	grog	8.5	13.5	0.5	engraved	Undetermined
F95-34	bone-grog	11.6	17.0	1.1	engraved	Nacogdoches Engraved
Bowl						
F31-4	bone-grog-hematite	8.3	12.7	0.4	plain	Undetermined
F31-15	grog	7.0	12.6	0.35	incised lines, effigy	Undetermined effigy vessel
F95-6	bone	5.0	15.5	0.3	engraved	Undetermined

Table 1. Vessels from the Washington Square Mound site (41NA49), cont.

Vessel No.	Temper	Height (cm)	Orifice Diameter (cm)	Volume (liters)	Decoration	Type
Bowl, cont.						
F95-10	grog-hematite	7.8	13.6	0.4	engraved	Nacogdoches Engraved
F95-18	grog-hematite	7.5	15.3-18.2	0.55	engraved	Nacogdoches Engraved
F95-25	grog-organics	8.5	14.0	0.5	engraved	Nacogdoches Engraved
Bottle						
F31-2	grog	23.0	6.3	0.65	engraved	Nacogdoches Engraved
F31-9	grog-hematite	17.5	6.1	0.6	engraved, red pigment	Nacogdoches Engraved
F95-23	grog	22.2	5.3	0.6	engraved, red pigment	Nacogdoches Engraved
F95-27	grog	15.5	4.7	0.5	engraved	Nacogdoches Engraved
Olla						
F31-12	grog	24.5	9.2	2.0	plain	Undetermined

Utility ware vessels are also well represented in the Washington Square Mound vessels from funerary contexts. Some are plain or undecorated (12.4%) (see Figure 7g), but the remainder are decorated with various wet paste designs, including brushed-punctated (12.4%, see Figures 7f and 8h, l), incised-punctated (10.2%, see Figure 8c-d, k), brushed-punctated-appliqued (4.1%, see Figure 8g), brushed-incised-appliqued-punctated (see Figure 8a), punctated (see Figure 7h), and incised elements and motifs.

Documentation of Associated and Unassociated Caddo Funerary Objects

Figure 7a. Selected vessel from Feature 31, F31-1.

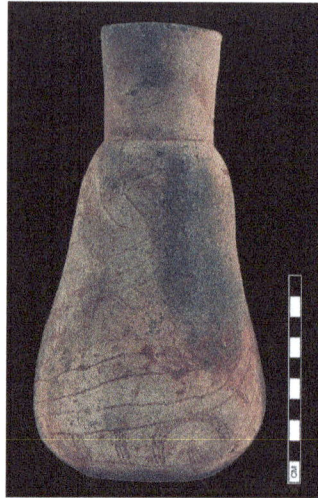

Figure 7b. Selected vessel from Feature 31, F31-2.

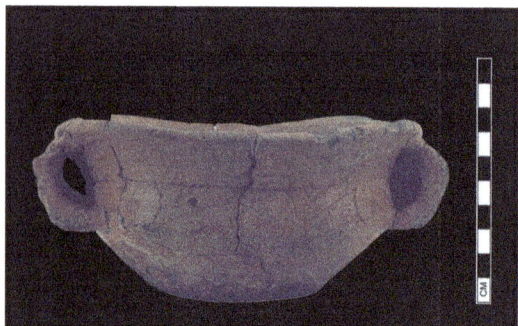

Figure 7c. Selected vessel from Feature 31, F31-3.

Figure 7d. Selected vessel from Feature 31, F31-5.

Figure 7e. Selected vessel from Feature 31, F31-9.

Figure 7f. Selected vessel from Feature 31, F31-10.

Figure 7g. Selected vessel from Feature 31, F31-12.

Figure 7h. Selected vessel from Feature 31, F31-14.

Figure 8a. Selected vessel from Feature 95, F95-4.

Figure 8b. Selected vessel from Feature 95, F95-8.

Figure 8c. Selected vessel from Feature 95, F95-11.

Figure 8d. Selected vessel from Feature 95, F95-13.

Documentation of Associated and Unassociated Caddo Funerary Objects

Figure 8e. Selected vessel from Feature 95, F95-14.

Figure 8f. Selected vessel from Feature 95, F95-19.

Figure 8g. Selected vessel from Feature 95, F95-20.

Figure 8h. Selected vessel from Feature 95, F95-21.

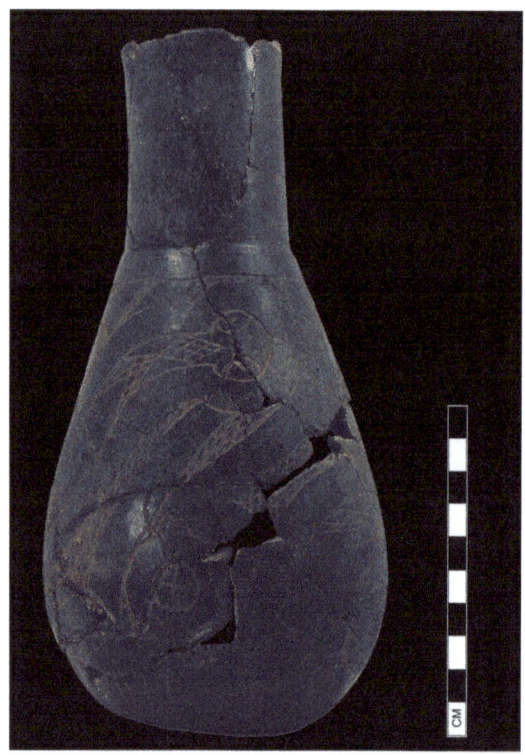

Figure 8i. Selected vessel from Feature 95, F95-23.

Figure 8j. Selected vessel from Feature 95, F95-27.

Figure 8k. Selected vessel from Feature 95, F95-28.

Figure 8l. Selected vessel from Feature 95, F95-33.

Documentation of Associated and Unassociated Caddo Funerary Objects

The principal resident Caddo pottery types at the Washington Square Mound site, as defined by Hart (1982), are Nacogdoches Engraved (n=15 vessels and one other vessel where the scroll motif is executed with punctations instead of engraved lines; we have labeled this vessel Nacogdoches Punctated), Washington Square Paneled (n=4), and Reavely Brushed-Incised (n=5). The Nacogdoches Engraved type is defined by distinctive engraved scrolls and several fill elements, including hatched triangles, narrow cross-hatched zones, small circles, and combinations of these elements (Hart 1982:46-48). Four of the Nacogdoches Engraved vessels have a pigment rubbed in the engraved lines, including red (n=2) in the carinated bowls and bottles and white (n=2) in the compound bowls. Reavely Brushed-Incised at the Washington Square Mound site is related to both Pease Brushed-Incised and Haley Complicated Incised because it has complicated brushed, incised, and/or appliqued fillet (i.e., the appliqued strip has been punctated) elements in panels on vessel bodies, sometimes also with punctated rows, that may be oriented vertically or in curvilinear patterns (Hart 1982:63 and Figure 3-9). Rims on Reavely Brushed-Incised tend to be brushed, with single rows of tool punctations under the lip and at the juncture of the rim and body (Hart 1982:65). Washington Square Paneled vessels have rectangular design elements comprised of rectangular panels "with straight or convex sides executed in incised, engraved, or punctated lines. The space between the sides of adjacent rectangles is filled with either punctations or diagonal incised or engraved lines. The tops and bases of the rectangles are straight, single, punctated, incised, or engraved lines. A single horizontal line is centered inside each rectangle and may or may not intersect the rectangles' sides" (Hart 1982:71-72).

At the Washington Square Mound site, Nacogdoches Engraved vessels occur on carinated bowls (n=4) (see Figure 8l, the Nacogdoches Punctated version of the type), compound bowls (n=5, see Figure 7a, c and Figure 8b), bowls (n=3), and bottles (n=4, see Figures 7b, e and 8i-j). Washington Square Paneled vessels include jars (n=1, see Figure 8d), carinated bowls (n=2, see Figure 8h), and compound bowls (n=1, see Figure 7d). The compound bowls at Washington Square have two distinct rim panels, usually with the lower panel being larger in width than the upper panel; on Late Caddo compound bowls, it seems to be the case that both panels are of equivalent width, but overall wider or taller than is the case with the Washington Square Mound compound bowls. All of the Reavely Brushed-Incised vessels are jars (see Figures 7f and 8a, g).

The remainder of the vessels from the Washington Square Mound burial features are of presently undetermined Caddo pottery types. The vessel shapes, decorations, temper inclusions, surface treatments, and firing conditions for these undetermined vessels are completely consistent with their having been made and used by Caddo groups that lived at the site (see Appendix 1). However, the identification of distinct ceramic types for most, if not all, Middle Caddo ceramic assemblages in East Texas, is currently poorly known. This is due at least in part to the considerable stylistic and formal diversity that characterizes Middle Caddo-aged ceramics across the region, as well as the absence of any serious effort to establish current and formally established ceramic type classifications. The Washington Square vessel and sherd assemblage would be a good place to start such an effort, but this is beyond the scope of the current project.

An equal proportion of decorated vessels of undetermined Caddo pottery type occur in both Feature 31 (40%) and Feature 95 (37.5%), suggesting the existence of a shared but stylistically diverse (if not also idiosyncratic) tradition of ceramic tradition at the Washington Square Mound site during the time both burials were interred in the Reavely-House Mound. In the case of the Feature 31, the majority of the undetermined type vessels are utility wares, while undetermined type engraved pottery is characteristic of the Feature 95 vessels, especially the decorations engraved on carinated bowls and compound bowls (see Table 1). Among the decorated jars, for instance, those undetermined to type are comprised of two incised-punctated, three brushed-punctated, and two tool punctated (see Figure 7h) vessels. Most of these are from Feature 31 (see Table 1). One of the undetermined type vessels from Feature 31 is a brushed-punctated carinated bowl (F31-11). There are five decorated carinated bowls from Feature 95 that are of undetermined type, including three that are engraved (see Figure 8f), one that has an engraved and rocker stamped design, and a fifth with an incised-punctated design on the vessel rim (see Figure 8c). Three of the compound bowls from Feature 95 have typologically unidentified engraved motifs (see Figure 8e). The one decorated bowl of undetermined type from Feature 31 is an incised effigy vessel (F31-15), and there is a single engraved bowl of undetermined type from Feature 95.

The plain ware vessels include one jar, three carinated bowls, one bowl, and one olla (see Table 1 and Figure 7g). The plain vessels are generally small to medium-sized in volume.

Two vessels from the Washington Square Mound site are not from clear funerary contexts. The first of these was found in 1957 with a burial in the historic Oak Grove Cemetery just southeast of the central part of the site (Figure 9a), but likely within the boundaries of the site as it existed in prehistoric times. According to Corbin (1980), this vessel was found with 15 small arrow points within it (see Appendix 7). The second was found in 1939 during work at what is now the northeastern corner of Thomas J. Rusk Middle School, less than 100 ft. southeast of Mound 1/2 (Corbin and Hart 1998:57). Corbin and Hart (1998:Figure 13) suggest this vessel (Figure 9b) has been reconstructed from parts of two or three different vessels, and there is no available evidence to indicate that it was found associated with a Caddo burial, only that it came from the heart of the mound center.

There are differences between the vessels from the two burial features at Washington Square Mound in several respects. First, the Feature 31 offerings include more jars (40%) and bottles (13.3%), while carinated bowls (43.8%) dominate the Feature 95 vessel assemblage. Proportionally, however, there is little variation in the occurrence of compound bowls (18.8-20.0%) or bowls (12.5-13.3%) in the two features; the one olla (see Figure 7g) is from Feature 31.

This feature vessel assemblage is also divergent in the relative proportions of fine wares, utility wares, and plain wares. More than 59% of the Feature 95 vessels are fine wares, compared to 33% (including the incised effigy vessel) in Feature 31. Utility ware vessels (47%) and plain ware vessels (20%) are more abundant in Feature 31 than they are in Feature 95: 31% utility ware vessels and 10% plain ware vessels. These differences in the character of the vessel funerary offerings, especially the high number of fine wares in Feature 95, as well as the very large number of vessels placed in the grave, may suggest that the individuals buried in this feature had a higher rank or status than the adult male Caddo in Feature 31, or that the lineages these individuals were associated with had different statuses.

Prehistoric and early historic Caddo mortuary ceramic assemblages differ "considerably from region to region within the Caddoan area in the composition of jars, bottles, bowls, and carinated bowls" (Perttula 2000:144). These differences are thought to be related to diverse social, religious, and philosophical beliefs held by different Caddo groups regarding the kinds of ceramic vessels important for use in life and also needed in the after-life (cf. Swanton 1942:205).

In an examination of more than 3000 mortuary vessels from Caddo sites in East Texas, northwestern Louisiana, and southwestern Arkansas (Perttula 2000: Table 7), the Washington Square Mound vessel assemblage in toto is quite distinctive because of the high proportions of carinated bowls and compound bowls (49%), and lesser amounts of cooking jars (28.6%), bowls (12.4%), and bottles (8.2%). The only mortuary vessel assemblage comparable to that of the Washington Square Mound burial vessels is that seen among Titus phase groups (dating from ca. A.D. 1430-1680, postdating the occupation at Washington Square) living in the Big Cypress Creek basin to the north. Both the Titus phase groups and the Washington Square Mound Caddo community had a strong need for food-serving vessels (particularly medium to large carinated bowls; compound bowls are more prevalent in the latter burials). Such was also the case among Frankston and Allen phase Caddo groups in the Neches and Angelina river basins, although these Caddo preferred carinated, globular, and shouldered bowls (55%).

Figure 9a. Other vessel from the Washington Square Mound site, from the Oak Grove cemetery, found in 1957.

Figure 9b. Other vessel from the Washington Square Mound site, brushed-punctated vessel reconstructed from parts of two or three vessels, found in 1939 on the grounds of what is now the T. J. Rusk Elementary School.

Documentation of Associated and Unassociated Caddo Funerary Objects

Cooking and storage jars are ubiquitous in both Washington Square and Titus phase (30%) vessel assemblages. The frequency of jars speaks to the importance of cooking and storage vessels for sustaining Caddo agricultural lifeways, and for ensuring that the individual or individuals in the graves had enough foodstuffs (placed in the jars, and probably also in baskets and bags that have decayed) for sustenance on his or her journey (see Swanton 1942:210).

Bottles were not as important as a burial offering for the Washington Square Mound burials (8.2%) as they are for other Caddo groups. In certain mortuary assemblages of Caddo burials from the Ouachita River basin in southwest Arkansas, the Little River basin, the lower Sulphur River in northeastern Texas, and in cemeteries along the Great Bend of the Red River, bottles comprise 23-42% of the ceramic mortuary offerings (Perttula 2000: Table 7). Other areas occupied by the Caddo where bottles did not feature strongly as burial offerings include the Titus phase (10%) and the Frankston-Allen phase (13%) areas of East Texas.

The sizes of the vessels placed in the two burial features are comparable (Table 2), except for the carinated bowls. There is only one miniature carinated bowl in Feature 31 but a range of small, medium, and large carinated bowls in Feature 95. In general, the vessels placed as funerary offerings in the Feature 31 and Feature 95 burials at Washington Square Mound are medium-sized in volume. Most of the variability in vessel sizes occurs in the Feature 31 jars and compound bowls and the Feature 95 carinated bowls.

Both the Feature 31 and Feature 95 vessels are primarily tempered with grog or crushed sherds, but frequently with other inclusions (Table 3), including crushed and burned bone, hematite, or charred organic remains. Vessels tempered only with grog are slightly more common in Feature 31, while vessels tempered only with bone are more prevalent in Feature 95. In general, bone and hematite were more commonly added as aplastics to the Washington Square Mound vessels interred with the two Caddo people in Feature 95 (Table 3).

Less than 10% of the vessels have a sandy paste, and less than 7% have charred organics present in the paste. Caddo vessels with sandy pastes tend to be utility wares used in every-day cooking and heating tasks, and thus the low frequency of sandy paste wares here is evidence of the fact that fine wares were preferentially and more commonly placed in the two burial features compared to jars. The low occurrence of charred organics in the paste of the Washington Square Mound vessels suggests that these vessels were well and evenly fired, and fired for a sufficient duration that any organics included in the paste were completely combusted.

Table 2. Vessel volume (in liters) comparisons by feature.

Vessel Form		Feature 31	Feature 95
Jar	Mean and SD	1.05 ± 0.43	1.20 ± 0.20
	CV*	40.9	16.7
	Range	0.7-1.9	0.9-1.5
Carinated bowl	Mean and SD	0.15	1.51
	CV	-	51.7
	Range	-	0.7-4.4
Compound bowl	Mean and SD	1.23 ± 0.58	1.16 ± 0.37
	CV	47.1	31.9
	Range	0.7-2.1	0.5-2.0
Bowl	Mean and SD	0.38 ± 0.035	0.44 ± 0.09
	CV	9.2	20.4
	Range	0.35-0.4	0.3-0.5
Bottle	Mean and SD	0.625 ± 0.025	0.55 ± 0.05
	CV	4.0	9.1
	Range	0.6-0.65	0.5-0.6
Olla	Mean	2.0	-

*CV=coefficient of variation

Table 3. Temper classes in the Feature 31 and 95 vessels.

Temper class	Feature 31	Feature 95
Grog	46.7*	37.5
Grog-hematite	20.0	18.8
Grog-bone	20.0	12.5
Grog-organics	0.0	3.1
Bone-grog-hematite	6.7	15.6
Bone	0.0	9.4
Bone-hematite	0.0	3.1
Bone-organics	6.7	0.0
% with grog	86.7	87.5
% with bone	33.4	40.6
% with hematite	26.7	37.5
% with organics	6.7	3.1
% with sandy paste	6.7	9.4
Total vessels	15	32

*percentage

The sherd assemblages from vessels used in non-mortuary contexts at the Washington Square Mound site indicate that grog was also the preferred temper for vessel manufacture (Hart 1982: Table 4-4). Sherds simply with grog account for 50.6% of the large sample (over 6000 sherds), roughly comparable to the 37.5-46.7% in the feature burials. Bone tempered sherds are less common in non-mortuary contexts (3.7%) than they are in either the Feature 31 (6.7%) or Feature 95 (12.5%) vessels, however. Conversely, grog-bone-tempered vessels account for 26.7-28.1% of the Feature 31 and Feature 95 vessels, respectively, but 45.6% of the sherds from non-mortuary contexts are grog and bone-tempered. From these data, it is reasonable to conclude that mortuary and non-mortuary vessel assemblages were not made and tempered the same, probably heavily influenced by the high numbers of engraved fine wares in the mortuary vessels and correspondingly higher amounts of plain and decorated utility ware vessels in the non-mortuary vessel sherds.

These compositional differences are further evident in the comparison of the proportions of different kinds of decorated fine wares and utility wares in both the funerary vessels and non-mortuary vessel sherds (Table 4). As Table 4 illustrates very well, engraved fine wares are almost seven times more prevalent in mortuary contexts than they are in non-mortuary contexts at the site, and clearly they were deliberately selected as a funerary accompaniment

Table 4. Decorated fine wares and utility wares in funerary vessels and non-mortuary vessel sherds from the Washington Square Mound site.

Wares	sherds from non-mortuary contexts*	mortuary contexts
Fine wares		
Engraved	8.2**	51.2
Engraved-punctated	0.1	2.3
Engraved-rocker stamped	0.0	2.3
Sub-total	8.3	55.8
Utility wares		
Brushed	54.7	0.0
Brushed-incised-punctated	0.2	2.3***
Brushed-incised	3.7	0.0
Brushed-punctated-appliqued	0.1	4.7
Brushed-punctated	3.6	14.0
Brushed-appliqued	0.6	0.0
Sub-total	62.9	21.0
Pinched	0.6	0.0
Incised	14.1	2.3
Incised-punctated	4.0	11.6
Punctated	9.9	9.3
Appliqued	0.3	0.0
Incised-appliqued	0.1	0.0
Sub-total	29.0	23.2
Total	5201 sherds	43 decorated vessels

*from Hart (1982) and Perttula (2009)
**percentage
***brushed-incised-appliqued-punctated (Reavely Brushed-Incised)

more often than any other kind of ceramic vessel. The engraved designs on these vessels likely had very specific social and ritual meanings to the Caddo lineages the deceased belonged to, as well as to the larger community that used the Washington Square Mound site for civic and ceremonial purposes.

Decorated utility wares, especially those with brushing (either as the sole decorative treatment or in combination with other decorative methods), are three times more common in non-mortuary contexts than they are as funerary offerings. In fact, almost 63% of all the decorated sherds have brushing (see Table 4). Incised, punctated, pinched, and appliqued sherds and vessels are roughly equivalent in frequency between mortuary and non-mortuary contexts, although incised vessel sherds are more common in the latter and incised-punctated vessels are more abundant in the former archeological contexts (see Table 4).

In summary, then, vessels in mortuary contexts at the Washington Square Mound site are predominantly engraved, brushed-punctated, and incised-punctated (see Table 4), accounting for more than 80% of the decorated vessels. In vessel sherds from non-mortuary contexts, the principal decorative methods are brushed, incised-punctated, and punctated; these account for almost 79% of the decorated sherds.

In addition to the differences already noted in vessel composition, proportion of fine wares, utility wares, and plain wares, as well as choices in temper selection, the vessels from Feature 31 and 95 were fired in different ways (Table 5). In the case of the Feature 31 vessels, 50% were fired in a high oxygen environment as compared to only 10.3% of the Feature 95 vessels. Almost 90% of the Feature 95 vessels were fired in a low oxygen or reducing environment (probably smothered in the coals), and most of these were subsequently removed from the fire to cool, leaving a thin oxidized layer along either interior and/or exterior vessel surfaces.

Table 5. Firing conditions observed in the Feature 31 and 95 vessels.

Firing conditions*	Feature 31	Feature 95
Oxidizing environment	20.0**	3.4
Incompletely oxidized	30.0	6.9
Reducing environment	10.0	13.8
Fired in a reducing environment, cooled in the open air	40.0	75.9
Total vessels	10	29

*follows Teltser (1993: Figure 2a-h)
**percentage

The meaning of these vessel firing differences between vessel offerings placed in the two mortuary features is presently obscure. Possibilities that may account for these differences include temporal or social changes in the technology of firing or preferences in the hardness and color of vessels of different sizes, functions, and decorative style; a greater learned or developed ability to control the firing temperature and the duration of firing by individual potters, or even personal, familial, or community-wide choices that dictated how fine wares, utility wares, and plain wares needed to be fired. Certainly also influencing the differences in firing detected between the two mortuary features were decisions made by the living descendants of the deceased about what kinds of pottery vessels were appropriate to place as funerary offerings in the mortuary features, and what pottery vessels were available for mortuary use.

Another distinctive characteristic of the Washington Square Mound site funerary vessels are certain rim treatments. This includes four vessels (F31-3, F31-5, F31-10, and F95-20, see Figures 7c-d, f and 8g) with rim peaks (including one with strap handles), one with a scalloped lip (F95-21, see Figure 8h), and four (F31-7, F95-6, F95-22, and F95-32, see Appendix 1) with a Redwine or pie-crust rim mode (Mark Walters, September 2007 personal communication). These rims are articulated (sometimes as much as at a 90 degree angle outward from the exterior vessel), and the lips are scalloped.

More than 8.5% of the vessels from Features 31 and 95 have rim peaks, another 8.5% have Redwine mode rims, and 2.1% have scalloped lips. Vessels with rim peaks are more abundant in the Feature 31 funerary vessels (20%) than in the Feature 95 vessels (3%), while Redwine mode rims are slightly more prevalent in Feature 95 (9.4%) than in Feature 31 (6.7%); the one scalloped rim vessel is from Feature 95.

Rim peak vessels include a Nacogdoches Engraved compound bowl, two Reavely Brushed-Incised jars, and one Washington Square Paneled compound bowl (see Table 1). The scalloped lip vessel is a Washington Square Paneled carinated bowl. Three of the four Redwine rim mode vessels are engraved—two carinated bowls, one identified as Nacogdoches Engraved, and the other an engraved bowl with a *Mode A* decoration (Hart 1982:78; Mode A rim sherds have been identified in Middle Caddo contexts at the Oak Hill Village site, see Rogers and Perttula [2004] in post-A.D. 1350 contexts)—and the other is a Reavely Brushed-Incised jar.

The Redwine rim mode was defined from vessels (n=2) and vessel rim sherds (n=2) at the Redwine site (41SM193, see Walters and Haskins 1998:Figure 11c, i). One of the vessels had engraved triangles on the flat rim as the only decoration, while the other was an engraved-punctated jar with strap handles. The prehistoric Caddo occupation at the Redwine site dates from A.D. 1304-1434.

This form of rim treatment has been identified at a few other sites in East Texas, from the middle Sabine River basin on the west and north, the Neches River basin to the west, and to the Attoyac Bayou basin on the east. This includes rim sherds or complete vessels from Washington Square Paneled vessels at 41SM196, 41SM223, and Leaning Rock (41SM325, Walters 2008) not far from the Redwine site, Washington Square Paneled vessels from 41SY41 (Tom Middlebrook, August 2007 personal communication) in the Attoyac Bayou basin, a

Washington Square Paneled carinated bowl from 41HS718 on the Sabine River (Gadus et al. 2006: Figure 4-40; the authors identified this vessel as a Glassell Engraved type), a Washington Square Paneled rim sherd from 41RK276 in the Martin Creek drainage (Sherman et al. 2001: Figure 32), and rim sherds from a minimum of eight Holly Fine Engraved and two Crockett Curvilinear Incised vessels at the George C. Davis site (41CE19) on the Neches River (Newell and Krieger 1949:Figures 30e, 35d, and 37a; Suhm and Jelks 1962:Plates 16g and 39g).

The distinctive rims at the George C. Davis site likely pre-date A.D. 1300, and may be the oldest known examples of this form of rim treatment. The other sites with the Redwine rim mode date from the mid- to late 13th century through the early part of the 15th century A.D, including the Washington Square Mound. The 2 sigma calibrated radiocarbon date from the Redwine site was mentioned above; the mean calibrated intercepts of radiocarbon dates from the Leaning Rock site is AD 1349, with a range from AD 1280-1420. At Washington Square, the primary Caddo occupation dates from ca. A.D. 1250-1425 based on four consistent calibrated dates from various non-mortuary features (Corbin and Hart 1998: Table 4). Although not a Redwine rim mode, Washington Square Paneled rim sherds—although not abundant—at the Oak Hill Village site (41RK214) are most common in the post-A.D. 1350 village (Rogers and Perttula 2004:258), providing further corroborating temporal evidence for the age of the Redwine rim mode. Taking this one step further, then, given that the Redwine rim mode is more common among the Feature 95 funerary vessels than the Feature 31 vessels, perhaps the Feature 95 shaft burial was placed in the Reavely-House Mound slightly later in time than the Feature 31 interment.

Clay Pigments

Clay and clay pigments of various colors were found in a number of vessels in both burial features. We know that hematite-rich red and a kaolin white clay pigments were rubbed in the designs of several of the engraved vessels, but the amounts of clay pigment placed in the vessels suggests these offerings were probably intended for use by the Caddo as body paints.

The following clay pigment offerings are in the SFA NAGPRA collections:
- dark greenish-gray glauconitic-rich clay above the foot of the Feature 31 burial
- black clay pigment (8 g), yellow pigment (16 g), and red pigment (4 g) inside Feature 95, Vessel 1
- yellow clay (150 g) inside Feature 95, Vessel 7
- red pigment (Figure 10) from Feature 95, Vessel 13 (40 g)
- reddish-brown to "purple" clay pigment (2 g) from Feature 95, Vessel 24
- white clay mixed with yellow clay (600 g) inside Feature 95, Vessel 30

Figure 10. Red clay pigment from Feature 95, Vessel 13.

Organic Remains

These materials represent the very poorly preserved remnants of organic materials placed in the Washington Square Mound burials that have almost completely rotted away through time. These organic remains probably included matting, baskets, hides, etc. A small amount of organic remains were in the SFA NAGPRA collections from Feature 95, found between Vessels 1 and 2/5 (see Figure 6), along with a possible mud dauber nest and 50 g of yellowish-red oxidized soil. There were also organic remains, mixed with a clay binding (20 g), inside Vessel 20 in Feature 95.

Marine Shell Beads

There are several concentrations of drilled marine shell columella beads from the burial features. These are cut from the central column of a Gulf Coast conch shell, and have a rectangular shape with flattened ends. In Feature 31, there was a cluster of shell beads at the wrist, two by the skull, and two others near what would have been the right leg of the Caddo man, perhaps attached to leggings.

In the wrist area (Table 6) of Feature 31, there are 11 mainly complete drilled columella beads, as well as 12 fragments (Figure 11a-c). In the area of the skull, the SFA NAGPRA collections include one fragmentary bead.

Documentation of Associated and Unassociated Caddo Funerary Objects

Table 6. Marine shell beads from Feature 31.

Context	Length (mm)	Exterior diameter (mm)	Drilled hole diam. (mm)
Wrist area			
	16.7	10.7	3.9
	12.8	9.8	2.8
	-	8.9	3.9
	16.0	11.6	4.0
	17.8	11.4	4.4
	18.0	9.1	4.3
	15.0	10.7	4.7
	16.1	10.1	-
	-	9.1	3.5
	17.0	9.0	5.3
	-	9.1	-

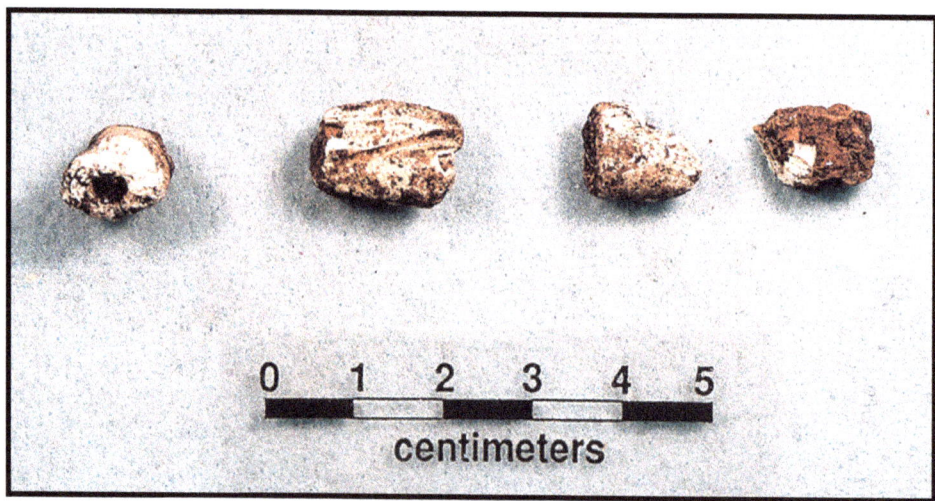

Figure 11a. Marine shell columella beads from the wrist area of Feature 31, lot 283.

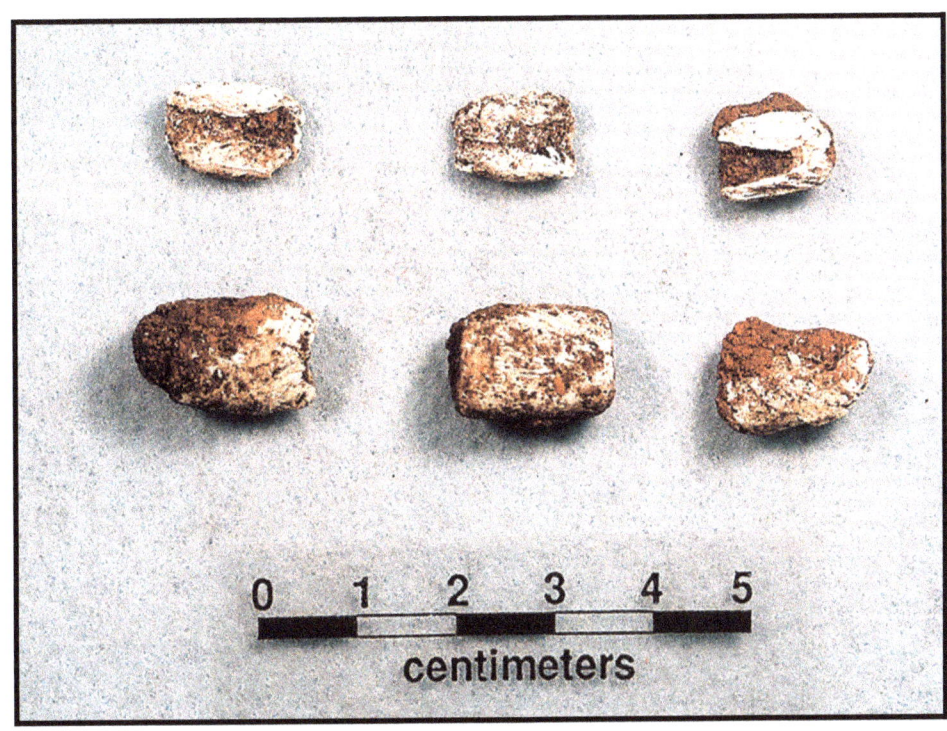

Figure 11b. Marine shell columella beads from the wrist area of Feature 31, F31-B, film canister 1.

Figure 11c. Marine shell columella beads from the wrist area of Feature 31, film canister 6, Cabinet 25.

In the case of Feature 95, there were clusters of drilled marine columella shell beads at the left and right wrists of the adult female (Burial-II). These include 20 more or less complete beads, six from the left wrist (Figure 12a) and 14 from the right wrist (Figure 12b), and 16 bead fragments (Table 7).

Table 7. Marine shell beads from Feature 95.

Context	Length (mm)	Exterior diameter (mm)	Drilled hole diam. (mm)
left wrist (B3)			
	15.9	9.0	3.9
	14.0	7.4	3.9
	16.9	10.0	3.4
	-	-	4.9
	15.9	10.2	3.9
	17.5	10.8	3.3
right wrist (B4)			
	15.5	9.7	3.8
	18.0	10.6	4.3*
	19.5	10.7	5.1*
	13.8	10.0	4.9
	17.0	8.1	4.2
	15.9	9.7	3.8
	16.1	9.0	4.0
	18.3	9.9	3.5
	15.0	11.7	4.1
	16.0	10.5	3.8
	-	10.9	4.4
	-	8.6	3.6
	17.1	10.5	3.8
	-	10.2	3.7

*These are the best preserved of all the marine shell beads at the site, and provide the best indication of the original size and shape of these offerings.

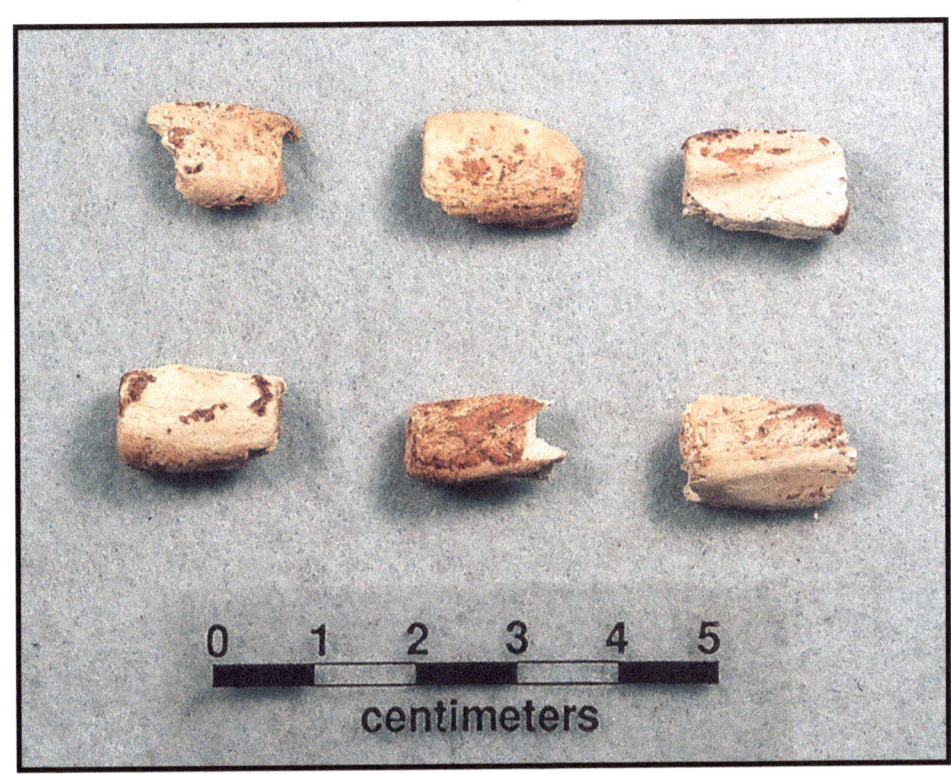

Figure 12a. Marine shell columella beads from Feature 95, left wrist.

Figure 12b. Marine shell columella beads from Feature 95, right wrist.

Marine Shell Pendant Fragment and Shell Disc Fragment

The marine shell pendant from Feature 95 is a 23 mm long piece, about 2.6 mm in thickness (Figure 13). It is impossible to discern any details of form or attachment from this poorly preserved piece, but its recovery from the chest area of the adult Caddo female indicates it was suspended around the neck at the time of her burial.

Figure 13. Marine shell pendant fragment from Feature 95.

The marine shell disc from Feature 95 is even more fragmented than the pendant, and is comprised of nothing more than a few miniscule shell fragments.

Deer teeth

Three deer teeth still encased in soil were recovered from Feature 31 from the wrist area of the deceased, the same area as a marine shell bead bracelet (see Figure 5). This suggests that some portion of a deer mandible had been placed as an offering with the deceased.

Lithic artifact cache

A cache of 11 lithic artifacts was found near the western end of the Feature 31 burial pit, next to Vessel 31-14. These artifacts, which include one core, nine unmodified pieces of lithic debris (soft hammer flakes), and one flake tool (Table 8 and Figure 14), probably represent part of a tool maker's kit that was put in a bag or container to accompany the deceased, and that bag eventually deteriorated over the years.

Table 8. Lithic Artifact Cache in Feature 31 at the Washington Square Mound site.

Lot No.	Raw material	cortex/type of cortex	comments
362	dark gray chert	present/limestone, roughened	flake fragment; non-local raw material
363	gray chert	present/smoothed	no platform grinding; bipolar flake
364	gray chert	present/smoothed	cortex on platform
365	gray chert	present/smoothed	crushed platforms; single platform core with six flake removals
366	gray chert	present/smoothed	cortex on platform; flake tool with unilateral use wear (29 mm in length)
367	grayish-brown chert	present/smoothed	no platform grinding
368	gray chert	present/smoothed	-
369	banded gray chert	present/smoothed	grinding on platform
370	gray chert	present/smoothed	cortex on platform
371	grayish-brown chert	present/smoothed	no platform grinding
372	gray chert	-	edge crushing

Figure 14. Lithic artifact cache from Feature 31.

The lithic artifacts in the cache consist of cherts, primarily gray (n=8, including the one core and one flake tool), grayish-brown (n=2), and dark gray (n=1) in color (see Table 8). The dark gray chert piece is likely from a Central Texas source (although such material is available in closer Trinity River and Neches River gravels, see Girard 1995; Banks 1990), based on its color and its roughened limestone-covered cortex. Nine of the 10 other lithic artifacts in the cache have smoothed and stream-rolled cortical remnants, and these were gathered by the Caddo from a stream gravel source, probably from either the Angelina or Neches rivers (Girard 1995:68-69).

The chert in these gravels primarily occurs as pebbles, although an occasional small cobble would have been available for procurement and use. As Caddo knappers were interested in obtaining flakes for tool manufacture (including flakes for arrow points, other formal tools, as well as expedient flake tools), rather than by the direct reduction of cores, the lithic artifact cache from Feature 31 apparently represented a stockpile of usable flakes for future tool manufacture, one ready-made flake tool (top row, third from left), and a single platform core (see Figure 14, left on the bottom row) that could be further reduced to obtain other flakes for tools.

41NA113

This site is on an alluvial terrace along the west side of La Nana Creek within the city limits of Nacogdoches, Texas. James E. Corbin recorded the site in 1977 on the basis of information from David Tucker, who found the site and uncovered a burial with funerary objects there; these funerary objects were subsequently donated to Stephen F. Austin University.

According to Corbin (1977 Site Survey Form), the site covered at least 100 m² and had been disturbed by road and railroad cuts. In addition to the one burial, there is a prehistoric occupational deposit at the site marked by Woodland period (ca. 500 B.C. to A.D. 800) sandy paste sherds and brushed and punctated Caddo pottery and a single dart point. There is also an early 19th century component at 41NA113 that has European decorated ceramics (transfer-printed, Mocha, hand-painted, and shell-edged ware).

The two vessels from 41NA113 are very small bowls (0.12-0.3 liters) with either direct or inverted rims and rounded lips, suggesting that they had been placed with the burial of a child. One is tempered with grog, and the other has no apparent temper inclusions. Their black to dark brown color also suggests that they were fired in a low oxygen or reducing environment.

The first vessel, has engraved concentric circles, repeated four times, that hook around a central circle; this may be a Taylor Engraved vessel. The other vessel is a distinctive Patton Engraved bowl. It has interlocking concentric circles below a single horizontal row of triangular tick marks under the vessel lip; white kaolin clay has been rubbed in the engraved design. Patton Engraved is the singular diagnostic ceramic artifact found on Historic Allen phase sites in the Angelina River basin (Fields 1995; Middlebrook 2007)

In addition to two ceramic vessels (see Appendix 4), there were three other funerary offerings in Burial 1. These include a 29.4 mm long *Olivella* marine shell bead with a longitudinal perforation (Figure 15), and two small (2.4 mm in diameter) round and light aqua glass beads. They are classified as IIa33 beads in the Kidd and Kidd (1970), and are a common bead type from 18th century Caddo contexts (Perttula 2005).

Figure 15. *Olivella* marine shell bead from 41NA113, Burial 1.

41PN48

The four vessels from 41PN48 (Appendix 5) were exposed in a burial in the Martin Lake Mine, probably that of a Caddo child based on the miniature size of the vessels (Espey, Huston & Associates, Inc. 1984b:40-51 and Figure 8a-d). There were no preserved human skeletal remains with the burial, which was exposed between 70-80 cm below surface in a gully cutting into a buried alluvial terrace.

The vessels from 41PN48 are all less than 0.5 liters in size. Two are brushed and two are plain. One of the brushed vessels is a bottle (PN48-1) with opposed brushing on the vessel body, an otherwise very unusual decorative treatment for Caddo bottles, and the other is a small jar (PN48-3) with horizontal brushing on the rim and vertical brushing on the vessel body. The occurrence of brushed vessels at 41PN48 suggests that the Caddo burial here dates from no earlier than ca. A.D. 1250, when brushing became a dominant surface decoration in many prehistoric Caddo ceramic assemblages in this general area (see Cliff and Perttula 2002:76-79). The other two vessels with the Caddo child included a plain carinated bowl (PN48-2) and a plain bowl (PN48-4).

Documentation of Associated and Unassociated Caddo Funerary Objects

The 41PN48 vessels were tempered with combinations of bone, grog, and hematite (see Appendix 5). Three of the four have grog and bone added to the paste, and all four vessels have crushed pieces of hematite; one of the vessels also has charred organic remains in the paste. In those instances where firing conditions could be ascertained, the brushed bottle was fired and cooled in a reducing or low oxygen environment, while the brushed jar was incompletely oxidized during firing.

41TT135

This site was first recorded in 1973 prior to the construction of Lake Monticello in the Big Cypress Creek basin (McCormick 1973:78). The site is on a sandy knoll along Smith Creek, a small tributary of Blundell Creek (Espey, Huston & Associates, Inc. 1984a:39-43, 78-98). It was not inundated by the lake, but is located within the Monticello-Winfield lignite mine.

41TT135 has a Caddo habitation deposit that covers about 7500 m^2 of the knoll. Test excavations were undertaken in 1982 to evaluate the research significance of the site before possible lignite mining would effect it. During that work, a prehistoric Caddo burial was exposed between 80-100 cm bs in a 85 x 55+ cm pit. There were no human remains preserved in the pit, but there was one broken ceramic vessel placed as a funerary offering in the pit (Appendix 6).

Excavations in the habitation area indicate that the prehistoric Caddo occupation at 41TT135 pre-dates A.D. 1400, and probably pre-dates A.D. 1200. This is based on the recovery of stemmed arrow points, Red River style long-stemmed pipe fragments (Espey, Huston & Associates, Inc. 1984a:Figure 14b), the relative paucity of decorated sherds (a plain: decorated sherd ratio of 2.75)—especially brushed sherds—a Holly Fine Engraved sherd (a ceramic type made by the Caddo between ca. A.D. 850-1300, see Story 2000), and the dominance of fingernail punctated sherds in the decorated sherd collection.

The plain vessel is a medium-sized bowl (volume of 1.1 liters). It has been tempered with bone and hematite, and was fired in a reducing environment, but then pulled from the fire to cool in a high oxygen environment.

41SY83

Espey Huston & Associates, Inc. recorded this site as part of their survey of the proposed Tenaha-Timpson transmission line right-of-way in Shelby County, Texas. The site is located on a natural sandy knoll adjacent to Ramsey Creek. Site size is estimated at 20 m in diameter, and archeological materials were recovered from three of seven shovel tests excavated within the project right-of-way where it crossed the knoll. Three complete prehistoric Caddo pottery vessels and one flake were recovered from Shovel Test 1 between 40-60 cm bs, while a single plain sherd was found in Shovel Test 4 (20-30 cm bs), and one lithic flake was found between 0-10 cm bs in Shovel Test 7 (Sundborg and Glander 1992:7-3).

41SY83 is a small Middle Caddo site with at least one isolated burial, based on the occurrence of three whole vessels in relatively deep contexts in a shovel test. No human remains were observed in that shovel test, but that is likely the product of the lack of preservation of the remains in the acidic sandy soils on the knoll. Whole vessels on prehistoric Caddo sites in East Texas in the vast majority (99.9% of the cases) of known cases are found only in burial features; the burial pit would not have been noticed in the excavation of a small shovel test.

The vessels from 41SY83 include an engraved bottle, a plain simple bowl, and a plain handled vessel—possibly a ladle or dish (see Appendix 8). All vessels from the site are grog-tempered.

Greasy Creek

The only information available about two vessels in the SFA NAGPRA collections is that they are from the Greasy Creek area of Camp County, Texas (see Appendix 3. This area is replete with large Late Caddo Titus phase cemeteries, the largest being the cemetery at the Shelby site (41CP71, see Perttula and Nelson 2004). This site has been the scene of extensive looting in the 1970s and 1980s, and we suspect—but cannot prove—that these vessels are from this site.

One of the two vessels is a Ripley Engraved bowl with an exterior folded lip. Ripley Engraved vessels are by far the most common engraved fine ware placed in Titus phase Caddo burials (see Perttula 2005, ed.: Table 11-10; Thurmond 1990). This particular vessel is very small in size (0.2 liters), fired and cooled in a reducing environment, and engraved on the rim with a circle and cross motif that is repeated five times around the vessel rim. The second vessel from the Greasy Creek area is a small (0.3 liters) plain carinated bowl tempered with grog and burned bone.

Unknown Caddo Burial Sites

Finally, there are three vessels from an unknown site or sites in East Texas (see Appendix 3), and there is virtually no information available about them in the SFA files. One of the vessels (Vessel 31.3), however, in the SFA collection was originally donated to the Stone Fort Museum, and there is an undated catalogue work sheet that accompanied it that indicates the vessel was found near Alto in Cherokee County, Texas. This vessel is a large (3.1 liters in volume) engraved and brushed carinated bowl; the vessel has horizontal brushing on the body, and the rim has sets of vertical engraved lines repeated three times around the rim.

The second vessel from an unknown East Texas Caddo burial site is a small plain bottle (Vessel 31.1) tempered with bone. The last vessel (Vessel 31.2) is an engraved compound bowl of the Wilder Engraved type, a common ceramic type in Late Caddo Titus phase contexts (cf. Perttula 2005, ed.; Thurmond 1990). It would not be out of place with the two Greasy Creek vessels in the SFA NAGPRA collections.

Chapter 3

NATIVE AMERICAN GRAVES PROTECTION AND REPATRIATION ACT (NAGPRA) FINDINGS AND RECOMMENDATIONS

In this report, we have documented funerary objects from a number of prehistoric archeological sites (dating between as early as ca. A.D. 1000 and the early 18th century) from several sites in northeastern and East Texas. The archeological evidence that has been reviewed in this study, and the documentation of the funerary objects from the various sites, have led to the following findings under NAGPRA for the Stephen F. Austin State University (SFA) NAGPRA collections:

- First, the funerary objects documented at the Washington Square Mound site (41NA49), the one whole vessel from the Oak Grove Cemetery (see Figure 9a) within the boundaries of the Washington Square site itself, 41NA113, 41PN48, 41TT135, 41SY83, and at least two unknown sites in Camp and Cherokee counties, Texas, as part of this study are from prehistoric Caddo burials. It is well known from archeological, bioarcheological, historical, archival, and oral historical records that the prehistoric Caddo are ancestral to the modern-day Caddo Nation of Oklahoma (Rogers and Sabo 2004: Figure 1), and the sites in question are situated within the ancestral territory of the Caddo people. Consequently, the funerary objects from these sites are culturally affiliated with the Caddo Nation of Oklahoma as defined in 25 U.S.C. 3001, Section 2 and Code of Federal Regulations, Title 43, Part 10, Section 10.2(e). These funerary objects include all offerings documented from Feature 31 and 95 at the Washington Square Mound site and the whole vessels from the other Caddo sites discussed above and documented in Appendix 3-6 and 8 of this report;

- Second, the preponderance of archeological evidence supports this finding, namely (a) the manner of burial practice when that information is available (i.e., in a pit where the body of a deceased Caddo individual was laid in the grave in an extended position with funerary objects placed around the body); (b) the kinds of funerary objects placed with the deceased, including culturally diagnostic and well-recognized Caddo pottery types; (c) the fact that whole pottery vessels on Caddo sites are, to a greater than reasonable certainty, from offerings from Caddo burial features; (d) the occurrence of the burials from these sites (with the exception of those from several unknown Caddo burial sites in Camp and Cherokee counties) in direct association with either Caddo habitation and mound features; (e) the use of Caddo style (cf. Derrick and Wilson 1997) cranial deformation in two burials from the Washington Square Mound site; and (f) more specific bioarcheological data from Washington Square (see Appendix 2) that is in concordance with general Caddo bioarcheological findings (Rose et al. 1998);

Documentation of Associated and Unassociated Caddo Funerary Objects

- Third, all the funerary objects from Features 31 and 95 at the Washington Square Mound site are considered to be associated funerary objects under NAGPRA (25 U.S.C. 3001, Section 2 (3)(a) and Code of Federal Regulations, Title 43 Section 10.2(d)(2)(i)). We reached this finding because the funerary objects from these features were found in direct association with preserved prehistoric Caddo human remains (see Appendix 2), and these remains are presently in the SFA NAGPRA collections;

- Fourth, because there are no human remains in the SFA NAGPRA collections (and none are known to exist in any other curation or museum facility) from 41NA113, 41PN48, 41TT135, 41SY83, or the unknown Caddo burial sites in Camp County (Greasy Creek area) or Cherokee County, Texas, the prehistoric Caddo funerary objects from these sites are considered unassociated funerary objects (25 U.S.C. 3001, Section 2 (3)(b) and Code of Federal Regulations, Title 43 Section 10.2(d)(2)(ii)); and

- Fifth, one of the vessels from the Washington Square Mound site (see Figure 9b)—from the Thomas J. Rusk Middle School built atop the Washington Square Mound site—is culturally affiliated with the Caddo Nation of Oklahoma, but the available archeological evidence in the totality of the circumstances is not sufficient to determine if the reconstructed vessel (possibly composed of two or three separate broken vessels found in 1939 that were joined during reconstruction, see Corbin and Hart [1998:57]), was associated with a Caddo burial. On this basis, we conclude that reconstructed Vessel 39.1 (Upton vessel) is not either an associated or unassociated funerary object under 25 U.S.C. 3001, Section 2 (3)(a-b) and Code of Federal Regulations, Title 43, Section 10.2(d)(2)(i-ii). If records or substantive information is uncovered in the future that sheds specific light on the archeological context of the discovery of Vessel 39.1 (Upton vessel)—particularly information concerning its discovery in association with Caddo human remains at the Washington Square Mound site—these findings under NAGPRA will need to be re-evaluated by SFA and the Caddo Nation of Oklahoma.

End Note

1. The vessel count presented here for Feature 95 differs from the 34 vessels mentioned by Hart (1982) and Corbin and Hart (1998:69). Vessels F95-2 and F95-5 are actually parts of the same vessel, and Vessels F95-19 and F95-24 are part of the same vessel. Furthermore, vessel F95-26 was incorrectly identified as vessel F95-24 by Hart (1982).

References Cited

Banks, L. D.
1990 *From Mountain Peaks to Alligator Stomachs: A Review of Lithic Sources in the Trans-Mississippi South, the Southern Plains, and Adjacent Southwest.* Memoir No. 4. Oklahoma Anthropological Society, Norman.

Brown, J. A.
1996 *The Spiro Ceremonial Center: The Archaeology of Arkansas Valley Caddoan Culture in Eastern Oklahoma.* 2 Vols. Memoirs No. 29. Museum of Anthropology, The University of Michigan, Ann Arbor.

Cast, R., T. K. Perttula, B. Gonzalez, and B. Nelson
2006 *Documentation of Caddo Ceramic Vessels from 41WD60, Wood County, Texas.* Historic Preservation program, Caddo Nation of Oklahoma, Binger, Oklahoma.

Cliff, M. B. and T. K. Perttula
2002 *Results of National Register Investigations Conducted on Site 41PN175, Panola County, Texas.* Document No. 010242. PBS&J, Austin.

Corbin, J. E.
1980 Excavations at Washington Square Mound Site 1979. Paper presented at the Caddo Conference, Texarkana, Texas.

Corbin, J. E. and J. P. Hart
1998 The Washington Square Mound Site: A Middle Caddo Mound Complex in South Central East Texas. *Bulletin of the Texas Archeological Society* 69:47-78.

Derrick, S. and D. Wilson
1997 Cranial Modeling as an Ethnic Marker among the Prehistoric Caddo. *Bulletin of the Texas Archeological Society* 68:139-146.

Espey, Huston & Associates, Inc.
1984a *Archaeological Site Evaluations: Monticello-Winfield Mine, Titus and Franklin Counties, Texas.* Document No. 82532. Espey, Huston & Associates, Inc., Austin.

1984b *Additional Cultural Resource Investigations: Martin Lake Mine, Tracts A, B, and C.* Document No. 83718. Espey, Huston & Associates, Inc., Austin.

Ferring, C. R. and T. K. Perttula
1987 Defining the Provenance of Red-Slipped Pottery from Texas and Oklahoma by Petrographic Methods. *Journal of Archaeological Science* 14:437-456.

References Cited (cont.)

Fields, R. C.
1995   Analysis of Native-Made Ceramics. In *The Deshazo Site: Nacogdoches County, Texas, Volume 2: Artifacts of Native Manufacture*, edited by D. A. Story, pp. 173-232. Studies in Archeology 21. Texas Archeological Research Laboratory, The University of Texas at Austin.

Gadus, E. F. and R. C. Fields
1996   *Ceramic Vessels from the Pleasure Point Site (41MR63), Marion County, Texas*. Technical Report No. 22. Prewitt and Associates, Inc., Austin.

Gadus, E. F., R. C. Fields, J. K. McWilliams, J. Dockall, and M. C. Wilder
2006   *National Register Testing of Seven Prehistoric Sites in the Sabine Mine's Area Q, Harrison County, Texas*. Reports of Investigations No. 147. Prewitt & Associates, Inc., Austin.

Sundborg, Greg and Wayne P. Glander
1992   *A Cultural Resources Survey of the Proposed Tenaha-Timpson Transmission Line Right-Of-Way, Shelby County, Texas*. Document No. 910621, Espey, Huston & Associates, Inc., Austin, Texas.

Girard, J. S.
1995   The Chipped Stone Collection: Technological, Functional, and Typological Analyses. In *The Deshazo Site: Nacogdoches County, Texas, Volume 2: Artifacts of Native Manufacture*, edited by D. A. Story, pp. 33-156. Studies in Archeology 21. Texas Archeological Research Laboratory, The University of Texas at Austin.

Gonzalez, B., R. Cast, T. K. Perttula, and B. Nelson
2005   *A Rediscovering of Caddo Heritage: The W. T. Scott Collection at the American Museum of Natural History and Other Caddo Collections from Arkansas and Louisiana*. Historic Preservation Program, Caddo Nation of Oklahoma, Binger, Oklahoma.

Hart, J. P.
1982   An Analysis of the Aboriginal Ceramics from the Washington Square Mound Site, Nacogdoches County, Texas. Master's thesis, Department of Anthropology, Northeast Louisiana University, Monroe.

Kidd, K. E. and M. A. Kidd
1970   *A Classification System for Glass Beads for the Use of Field Archaeologists*. Canadian Historic Sites: Occasional Papers in Archaeology and History No. 1, pp. 45-89. National Historic Sites Service, National and Historic Parks Branch, Department of Indian Affairs and Northern Development, Ottawa, Ontario.

References Cited (cont.)

Middlebrook, T.
2007 A Survey of Historic Caddo Sites in Nacogdoches County. *Journal of Northeast Texas Archaeology* 26:99-115.

Newell, H. P. and A. D. Krieger
1949 *The George C. Davis Site, Cherokee County, Texas.* Memoirs No. 5. Society for American Archaeology, Menasha, Wisconsin.

Perttula, T. K.
2000 Functional and Stylistic Analyses of Ceramic Vessels from Mortuary Features at a 15th and 16th Century Caddo Site in Northeast Texas. *Midcontinental Journal of Archaeology* 25(1):101-151.

2004 The Prehistoric and Caddoan Archeology of the Northeast Texas Pineywoods. In *The Prehistory of Texas*, edited by T. K. Perttula, pp. 370-407. Texas A&M University Press, College Station.

2005 41HO64/65, Late 17th to Early 18th Century Caddo Sites on San Pedro Creek in Houston County, Texas. *Bulletin of the Texas Archeological Society* 75:85-103.

2009 Analysis of the Caddo Archeological Materials from the 1985 Texas Archeological Society Field School at the Washington Square Mound Site, Nacogdoches County, Texas. *Bulletin of the Texas Archeological Society* 80:145-193.

Perttula, T. K. (editor)
2005 *Archeological Investigations at the Pilgrim's Pride Site (41CP304), a Titus Phase Community in the Big Cypress Creek Basin, Camp County, Texas.* 2 Vols. Report of Investigations No. 30. Archeological & Environmental Consultants, LLC, Austin.

Perttula, T. K. and B. Nelson, with contributions by J. P. Dering, L. Schniebs, R. L. Turner, Jr., M. Walters, and D. Wilson
2004 *Archeological Investigations at the Shelby Site (41CP71) on Greasy Creek, Camp County, Texas.* Special Publication No. 5. Friends of Northeast Texas Archaeology, Pittsburg and Austin.

Perttula, T. K., R. Cast, B. Gonzalez, and B. Nelson
2008 *Documentation of Unassociated and Culturally Unidentifiable Funerary Objects in the U.S. Army Corps of Engineers, Fort Worth District Collections Housed at the Texas Archeological Research Laboratory at The University of Texas at Austin.* Historic Preservation Program, Caddo Nation of Oklahoma, Binger, Oklahoma.

References Cited (cont.)

Perttula, T. K., M. Tate, H. Neff, M. D. Glascock, E. Skokan, S. Mulholland, R. Rogers, and B. Nelson
1998 *Analysis of the Titus Phase Mortuary Assemblage at the Mockingbird or "Kahbakayammaahin" Site (41TT550)*. Document No. 970849. Espey, Huston & Associates, Inc., Austin.

Rice, P. M.
1987 *Pottery Analysis: A Sourcebook*. University of Chicago Press, Chicago.

Rogers, J. D. and G. Sabo III
2004 Caddo. In *Southeast, Volume 14 of the Handbook of North American Indians*, edited by R. D. Fogelson, pp. 616-631. Smithsonian Institution, Washington, D.C.

Rogers, R. and T. K. Perttula
2004 *The Oak Hill Village Site (41RK214), Rusk County, Texas*. Document No. 030083. PBS&J, Austin.

Rose, J. C., M. P. Hoffman, B. A. Burnett, A. M. Harmon, and J. E. Barnes
1998 Skeletal Biology of the Prehistoric Caddo. In *The Native History of the Caddo: Their Place in Southeastern Archeology and Ethnohistory*, edited by T. K. Perttula and J. E. Bruseth, pp. 113-126. Studies in Archeology 30. Texas Archeological Research Laboratory, The University of Texas at Austin.

Sherman, D. L., T. K. Perttula, S. S. Victor, and M. A. Nash
2001 *NRHP Eligibility Testing (41RK107, 41RK240, 41RK242, 41RK243, 41RK276, and 41RK286) and Additional Testing (41RK243) Investigations within the Oak Hill DIII Mine, Permit No. 46, Rusk County, Texas*. Document No. 00237. PBS&J, Austin.

Skibo, J. M.
1992 *Pottery Function: A Use-Alteration Perspective*. Plenum Press, New York.

Story, D. A.
1990 Cultural History of the Native Americans. In *The Archeology and Bioarcheology of the Gulf Coastal Plain*, by D. A. Story, J. A. Guy, B. A. Burnett, M. D. Freeman, J. C. Rose, D. G. Steele, B. W. Olive, and K. J. Reinhard, pp. 163-366. 2 Vols. Research Series No. 38. Arkansas Archeological Survey, Fayetteville.

2000 Introduction. In *The George C. Davis Site, Cherokee County, Texas*, by H. P. Newell and A. D. Krieger, pp. 1-31. 2nd Edition. Society for American Archaeology, Washington, D.C.

References Cited (cont.)

Suhm, D. A. and E. B. Jelks (editor)
1962 *Handbook of Texas Archeology: Type Descriptions.* Special Publication No. 1, Texas Archeological Society, and Bulletin No. 4, Texas Memorial Museum, Austin.

Swanton, J. R.
1942 *Source Material on the History and Ethnology of the Caddo Indians.* Bulletin 132. Bureau of American Ethnology, Smithsonian Institution, Washington, D.C.

Teltser, P. A.
1993 An Analytic Strategy for Studying Assemblage-Scale Ceramic Variation: A Case Study from Southeast Missouri. *American Antiquity* 58(3):530-543.

Thurmond, J. P.
1990 *Archeology of the Cypress Creek Drainage Basin, Northeastern Texas and Northwestern Louisiana.* Studies in Archeology No. 5. Texas Archeological Research Laboratory, The University of Texas at Austin.

Walters, M.
2006 The Lake Clear (41SM243) Site and *Crotalus horridus atricaudatus. Caddo Archeology Journal* 15:5-39.

Walters, M. with contributions from L. G. Cecil, L. S. Cummings, J. P. Dering, J. R. Ferguson, M. D. Glascock, T. K. Perttula, L. Schniebs, H. J. Shafer, J. Todd, and C. P. Walker
2008 Life on Jackson Creek, Smith County, Texas: Archeological Investigations of a 14TH Century Caddo Domicile at the Leaning Rock Site (41SM325). *Caddo Archeology Journal*, 18:1-114

Walters, M. and P. Haskins, with contributions by D. H. Jurney, S. E. Goldborer, and T. K. Perttula
1998 Archaeological Investigations at the Redwine Site (41SM193), Smith County, Texas. *Journal of Northeast Texas Archaeology* 11:1-38.

Appendix 1

**Vessel Recordation Forms
Washington Square Mound Site (41NA49)
NAGPRA Collections**

Documentation of Associated and Unassociated Caddo Funerary Objects

SITE NO.: 41NA49, Oak Grove Cemetery (southeast of the main portions of the site, Hart 1982:91)

FEATURE: -

VESSEL NO.: 31.6

NON-PLASTICS: grog

VESSEL FORM: Jar (reconstructed) with a direct rim and a rounded lip

CORE COLOR: G (reduced in a low oxygen environment and cooled in the open air)

INTERIOR SURFACE COLOR: strong brown (7.5YR 5/8)

EXTERIOR SURFACE COLOR: strong brown (7.5 YR 5/6)

WALL THICKNESS: 5.6 mm

INTERIOR SURFACE TREATMENT: burnished on rim and upper body

EXTERIOR SURFACE TREATMENT: smoothed on rim panels; fire clouds on the base

HEIGHT: 17.7 cm

ORIFICE DIAMETER: 14.5 cm

DIAMETER AT BOTTOM OF RIM OR NECK: 17.7 cm

BASE DIAMETER: 8.5 cm

ESTIMATED VOLUME: 2.3 liters

DECORATION: There are six diagonal incised panels on the rim, and each panel has curvilinear or semi-circular incised zones filled with tool punctates. Three of the wider panels have a central incised circle filled with punctations, while the three narrower others have four semi-circular or linear sets of incised zones filled with tool punctates (Figure 16).

TYPE: Undetermined incised-punctated utility ware vessel (Corbin and Hart 1998:Figure 5; Hart 1982:Figure 3-16a).

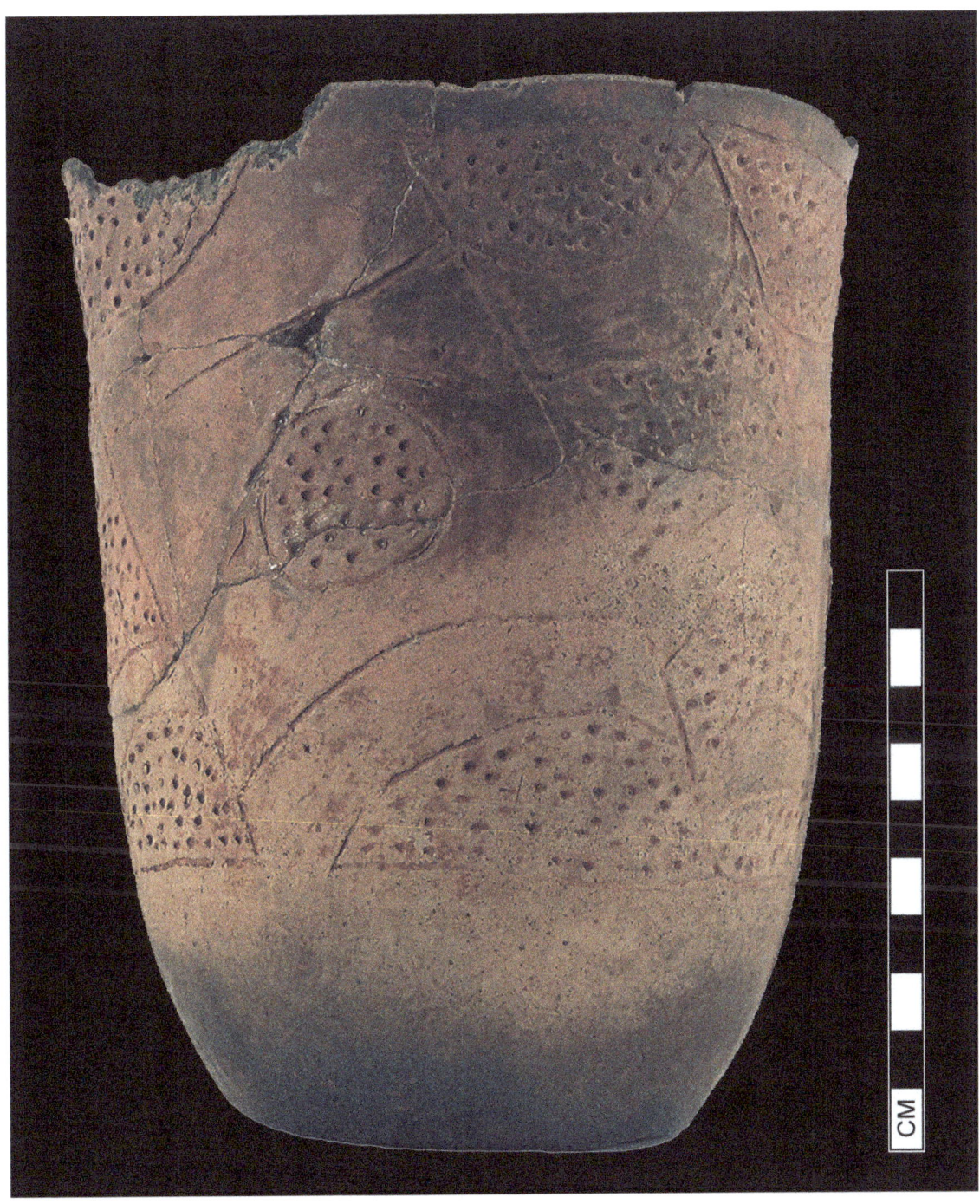

Figure 16. Incised-punctated utility ware vessel from the Washington Square Mound site, found at the Oak Grove Cemetery.

SITE NO.: 41NA49

FEATURE: -

VESSEL NO.: 39.1 (Upton vessel), found at the northeastern corner of T. J. Rusk Middle School

NON-PLASTICS: bone and hematite

VESSEL FORM: Jar (reconstructed) with everted rim and flat lip

CORE COLOR: Undetermined

INTERIOR SURFACE COLOR: black (10YR 3/1) on rim, otherwise brown (10YR 4/2)

EXTERIOR SURFACE COLOR: brown (10YR 4/2)

WALL THICKNESS: 8.9 mm at the rim

INTERIOR SURFACE TREATMENT: none

EXTERIOR SURFACE TREATMENT: none

HEIGHT: 34.0 cm

ORIFICE DIAMETER: 25.5 cm

DIAMETER AT BOTTOM OF RIM OR NECK: 19.5 cm

BASE DIAMETER: 13.0 cm

ESTIMATED VOLUME: 11.2 liters

DECORATION: The rim has seven horizontal rows of tool punctations, while the jar body has overlapping brushing marks (Figure 17).

TYPE: Undetermined brushed-punctated utility ware vessel (Corbin and Hart 1998: Figure 13).

Figure 17. Brushed-punctated utility ware vessel found on the grounds of the T. J. Rusk Middle School on the Washington Square Mound site.

Documentation of Associated and Unassociated Caddo Funerary Objects

SITE NO.: 41NA49

FEATURE: 31

VESSEL NO.: F31-1

NON-PLASTICS: grog

VESSEL FORM: Compound bowl with a direct rim, and a rounded and exterior folded lip

CORE COLOR: A (fired and cooled in an oxidizing environment)

INTERIOR SURFACE COLOR: brown (10YR 4/3)

EXTERIOR SURFACE COLOR: yellowish-brown (10YR 5/4) with black fire clouding, or a remnant of a black slip (Hart 1982:49)

WALL THICKNESS: 5.0 mm

INTERIOR SURFACE TREATMENT: burnished

EXTERIOR SURFACE TREATMENT: burnished

HEIGHT: 7.5 cm

ORIFICE DIAMETER: 11.8 cm

DIAMETER AT BOTTOM OF RIM OR NECK: 10.1 cm

BASE DIAMETER: 6.3 cm

ESTIMATED VOLUME: 0.7 liters

DECORATION: The two panels of the compound bowl have distinct engraved motifs (Figure 18). The upper panel has 12 pairs of upper and lower hatched triangular zones pendant from horizontal engraved lines; the lower hatched triangular zone is midway along the panel. The lower panel has two sets of scrolls (what Hart [1982:49] refers to as the *Crockett* scroll) comprised of narrow diagonal hatched zones with either attached hatched or cross-hatched curvilinear zones. These sets are divided by a single diagonal line with hatched triangles on either side of the line.

TYPE: Nacogdoches Engraved (Hart 1982: Figure 3-5a).

Figure 18. Nacogdoches Engraved compound bowl, F31-1.

Documentation of Associated and Unassociated Caddo Funerary Objects

SITE NO.: 41NA49

FEATURE: 31

VESSEL NO.: F31-2

NON-PLASTICS: grog

VESSEL FORM: Bottle with a slightly flaring neck, a direct rim and a flat lip, and a globular body

CORE COLOR: G (fired in a reducing environment, but cooled in the open air)

INTERIOR SURFACE COLOR: Undetermined

EXTERIOR SURFACE COLOR: pink (7.5YR 7/3), with fire clouding

WALL THICKNESS: 6.6 cm

INTERIOR SURFACE TREATMENT: none

EXTERIOR SURFACE TREATMENT: burnished

HEIGHT: 23.0 cm

ORIFICE DIAMETER: 6.3 cm

DIAMETER AT BOTTOM OF RIM OR NECK: 6.4 cm

BASE DIAMETER: 7.0 cm

ESTIMATED VOLUME: 0.65 liters

DECORATION: The bottle body has a complicated engraved scroll motif (with three or four curvilinear lines) that curves around the vessel, repeating itself twice; the central part of the scroll are engraved ovals (Figure 19). Dividing the scrolls are semi-circular, vertical, and engraved arcs, and engraved semi-circles and hatched triangles are employed to demarcate the repeated curvilinear scrolls from the top and bottom of the vessel body.

TYPE: Nacogdoches Engraved (Hart 1982: Figure 3-7d).

Figure 19. Nacogdoches Engraved bottle, F31-2.

Documentation of Associated and Unassociated Caddo Funerary Objects

SITE NO.: 41NA49

FEATURE: 31

VESSEL NO.: F31-3

NON-PLASTICS: grog and hematite

VESSEL FORM: Shouldered or compound bowl with an everted rim and a rounded lip. There are four rim peaks and two massive strap handles are attached to the rim (Figure 20).

CORE COLOR: E (incompletely oxidized during firing)

INTERIOR SURFACE COLOR: reddish-brown (5YR 4/4)

EXTERIOR SURFACE COLOR: yellowish-red (5YR 4/6), with a possible red (2.5YR 5/8) slip

WALL THICKNESS: 5.8 mm

INTERIOR SURFACE TREATMENT: burnished

EXTERIOR SURFACE TREATMENT: burnished

HEIGHT: 6.5 cm

ORIFICE DIAMETER: 16.5 cm

DIAMETER AT BOTTOM OF RIM OR NECK: 14.0 cm

BASE DIAMETER: 7.5 cm

ESTIMATED VOLUME: 0.9 liters

DECORATION: There are two panels on the vessel. The upper panel has four horizontal engraved lines, while the lower panel has a continuous scroll around small excised circles or dots (see Figure 20). A white clay pigment has been rubbed in the engraved lines. The strap handles are decorated with vertical engraved scrolls that wrap around an appliqued node centered on the handle. There are also cross-hatched fields and negative zones on either side of the strap handle's scroll.

TYPE: Nacogdoches Engraved (Hart 1982: Figure 3-5b).

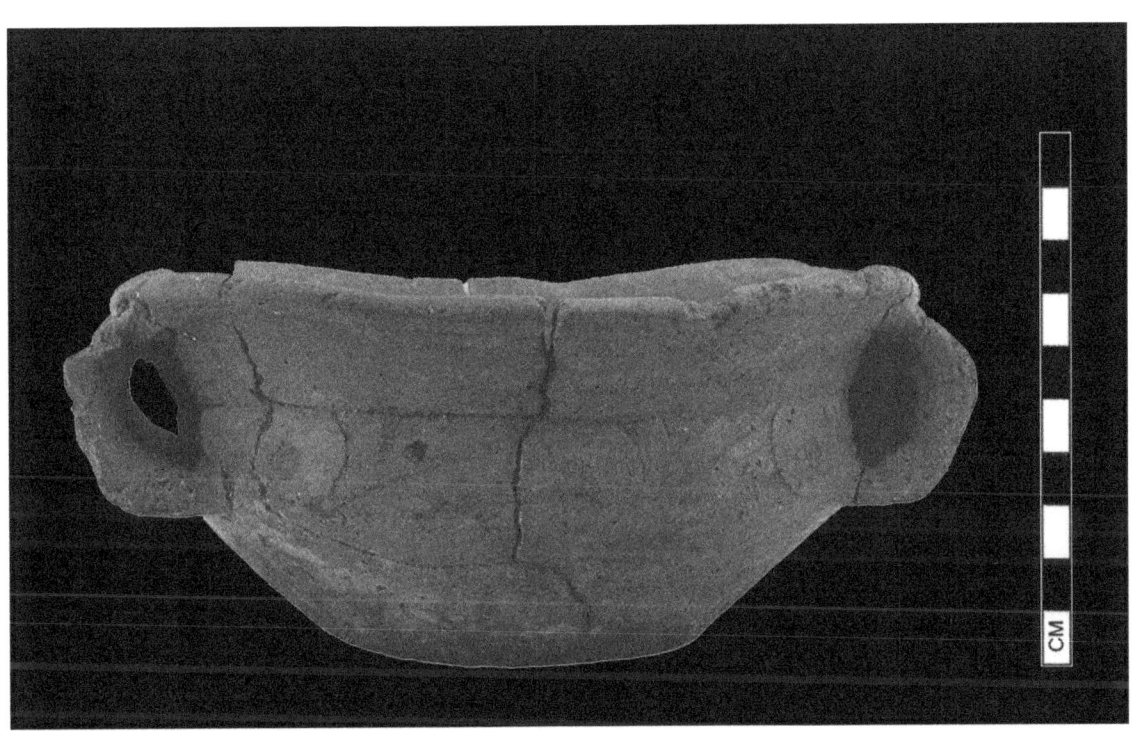

Figure 20. Nacogdoches Engraved compound bowl, F31-3.

Documentation of Associated and Unassociated Caddo Funerary Objects

SITE NO.: 41NA49

FEATURE: 31

VESSEL NO.: F31-4

NON-PLASTICS: bone, hematite, and grog

VESSEL FORM: Bowl with a inverted rim and a ground-down flat lip (Figure 21).

CORE COLOR: F (fired in a reducing environment but cooled in the open air)

INTERIOR SURFACE COLOR: brown (10YR 4/3)

EXTERIOR SURFACE COLOR: dark grayish-brown (10YR 4/2)

WALL THICKNESS: 5.9 mm

INTERIOR SURFACE TREATMENT: smoothed

EXTERIOR SURFACE TREATMENT: burnished

HEIGHT: 8.3 cm

ORIFICE DIAMETER: 12.7 cm

DIAMETER AT BOTTOM OF RIM OR NECK: N/A

BASE DIAMETER: 9.1 cm

ESTIMATED VOLUME: 0.4 liters

DECORATION: Plain

TYPE: Undetermined; this vessel appears to have been recycled from a previously broken vessel prior to its being placed in Feature 31 (Hart 1982:86-87).

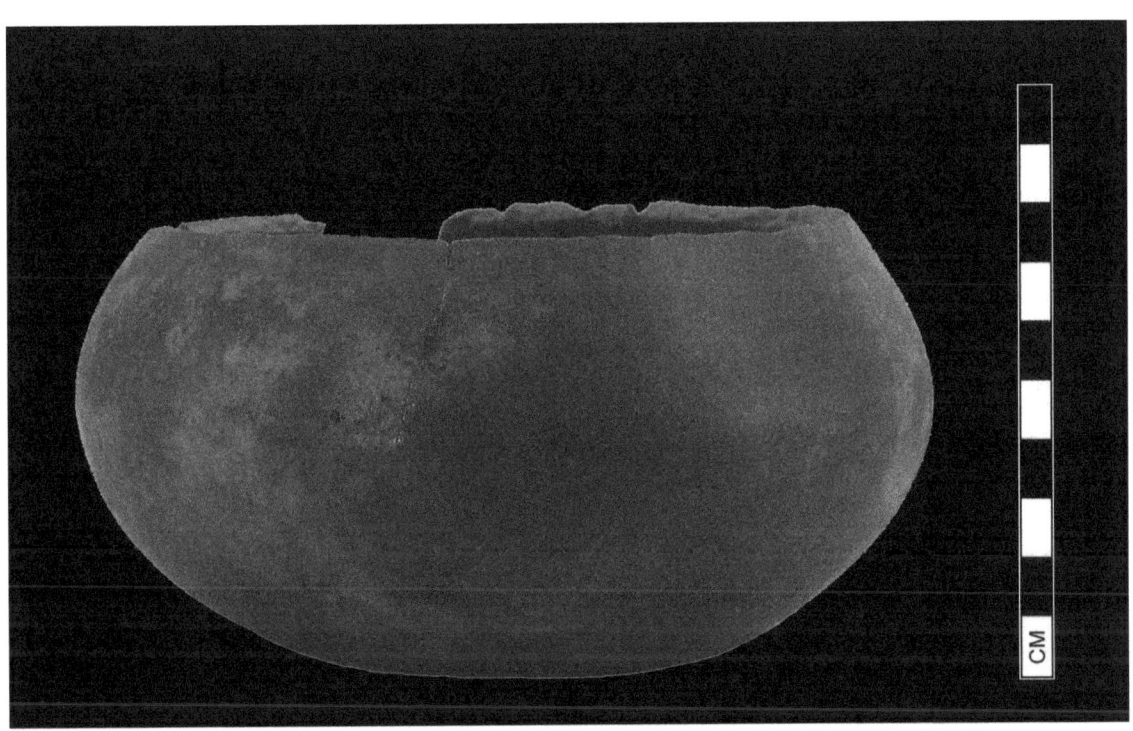

Figure 21. Plain bowl, F31-4.

Documentation of Associated and Unassociated Caddo Funerary Objects

SITE NO.: 41NA49

FEATURE: 31

VESSEL NO.: F31-5

NON-PLASTICS: grog

VESSEL FORM: Compound bowl with an everted rim and a rounded lip; the vessel also has four rim peaks

CORE COLOR: F (fired in a reducing environment and cooled in the open air)

INTERIOR SURFACE COLOR: brown (7.5YR 4/4)

EXTERIOR SURFACE COLOR: brown (7.5YR 4/4)

WALL THICKNESS: 6.2 mm

INTERIOR SURFACE TREATMENT: burnishing on the upper rim panel; the vessel body is pitted

EXTERIOR SURFACE TREATMENT: burnished

HEIGHT: 10.6 cm

ORIFICE DIAMETER: 25.0 cm

DIAMETER AT BOTTOM OF RIM OR NECK: 24.2 cm

BASE DIAMETER: 8.0 cm

ESTIMATED VOLUME: 2.1 liters

DECORATION: The upper vessel panel has eight hour glass-shaped punctated dividers set beneath or between each of the rim peaks. The lower vessel panel has both punctated dividers that are offset from those on the upper panel, as well as upper and lower punctated zones or panels (six in number), and a single central horizontal engraved line within each zone or panel (Figure 22).

TYPE: Washington Square Paneled (Hart 1982:Figure 3-12b).

Figure 22. Washington Square Paneled compound bowl, F31-5.

SITE NO.: 41NA49

FEATURE: 31

VESSEL NO.: F31-6

NON-PLASTICS: bone and grog

VESSEL FORM: Jar or Olla; the rim is missing

CORE COLOR: B (fired and cooled in a reducing environment)

INTERIOR SURFACE COLOR: light yellowish-brown (10YR 6/4)

EXTERIOR SURFACE COLOR: light yellowish-brown (10YR 6/4) with charred organic residues

WALL THICKNESS: 6.7 mm

INTERIOR SURFACE TREATMENT: burnished

EXTERIOR SURFACE TREATMENT: smoothed

HEIGHT: N/A

ORIFICE DIAMETER: N/A

DIAMETER AT BOTTOM OF RIM OR NECK: N/A

BASE DIAMETER: 9.8 cm

ESTIMATED VOLUME: Undetermined

DECORATION: Broad stroke vertical brushing or incising on the body, and the brushing is defined at the bottom by a single horizontal incised line (Figure 23). There is a single row of slash or linear punctates above this line, but in the brushed zone on the vessel.

TYPE: Undetermined brushed-incised-punctated utility ware vessel. Hart (1982:85 and Figure 3-15a) considered the vessel to have been incised rather than brushed.

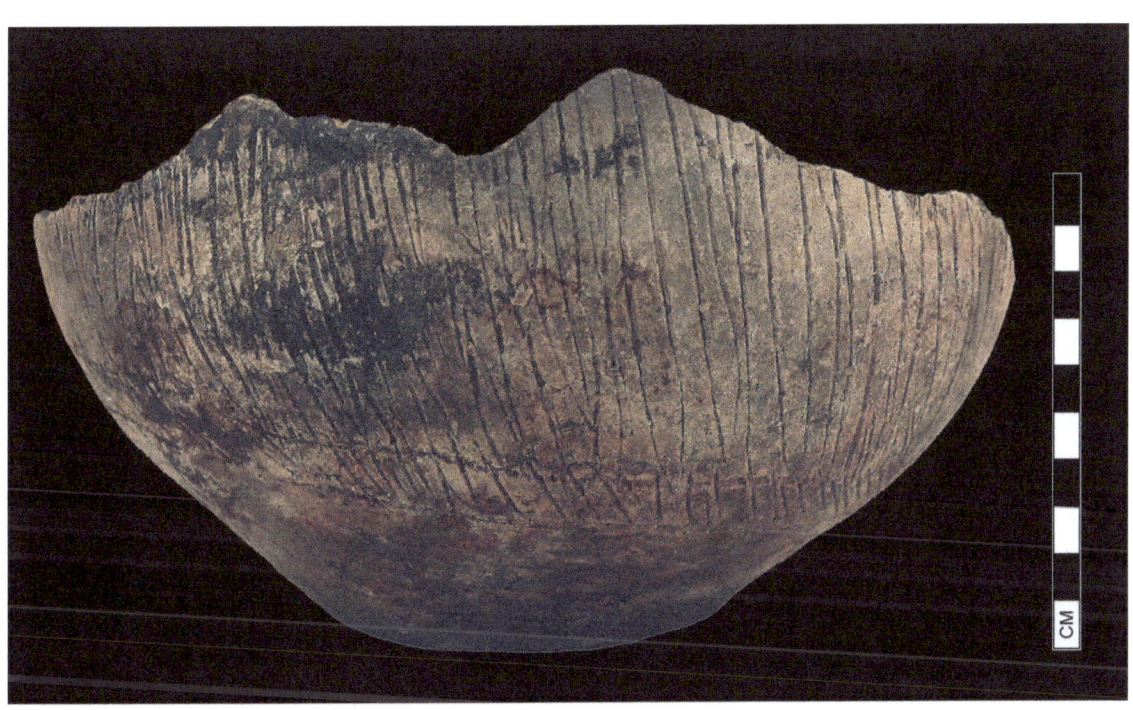

Figure 23. Brushed-incised-punctated utility ware vessel, F31-6.

Documentation of Associated and Unassociated Caddo Funerary Objects

SITE NO.: 41NA49

FEATURE: 31

VESSEL NO.: F31-7

NON-PLASTICS: bone-grog

VESSEL FORM: Jar with an everted rim and a pie-crust rim (i.e., flat on top and folded over at almost a 90 degree angle from the rim)

CORE COLOR: E (incompletely oxidized during firing)

INTERIOR SURFACE COLOR: yellowish-red (5YR 4/6)

EXTERIOR SURFACE COLOR: yellowish-red (5YR 4/6) with black fire clouding

WALL THICKNESS: 6.8 mm

INTERIOR SURFACE TREATMENT: burnished

EXTERIOR SURFACE TREATMENT: smoothed at the rim-body juncture

HEIGHT: 12.2 cm

ORIFICE DIAMETER: 18.0 cm

DIAMETER AT BOTTOM OF RIM OR NECK: Undetermined

BASE DIAMETER: 10.0 cm

ESTIMATED VOLUME: 1.9 liters

DECORATION: The rim has a zone of slash punctates under the vessel lip. The body has vertical brushing in eight panels separated by vertical appliqued fillets; these panels extend from the rim-body juncture to just above the base. There are also vertical rows of small punctations on the body within each of the brushed-appliqued panels (Figure 24).

TYPE: Reavely Brushed-Incised (Hart 1982: Figure 3-10a).

Figure 24. Reavely Brushed-Incised jar vessel section, F31-7.

Documentation of Associated and Unassociated Caddo Funerary Objects

SITE NO.: 41NA49

FEATURE: 31

VESSEL NO.: F31-8

NON-PLASTICS: hematite and grog

VESSEL FORM: Compound jar with the rim missing

CORE COLOR: Undetermined

INTERIOR SURFACE COLOR: dark brown (10YR 3/3)

EXTERIOR SURFACE COLOR: brown (10YR 4/3) to dark brown (10YR 3/3)

WALL THICKNESS: 6.2 mm

INTERIOR SURFACE TREATMENT: burnished

EXTERIOR SURFACE TREATMENT: none

HEIGHT: Undetermined

ORIFICE DIAMETER: Undetermined

DIAMETER AT BOTTOM OF RIM OR NECK: 12.0 cm

BASE DIAMETER: 8.9 cm

ESTIMATED VOLUME: Undetermined, but estimated greater than 2 liters

DECORATION: The upper vessel section of the jar has vertical brushing marks, while the lower jar section of the compound vessel has a horizontal row of tool punctates at what would be the rim-body juncture, and vertical brushing on the vessel body. The vertical brushing on the lower jar body is divided by rows of vertical tool punctates into six panels (Figure 25).

TYPE: Reavely Brushed-Incised brushed-punctated utility ware vessel (Hart 1982: Figure 3-10c).

Figure 25. Reavely Brushed-Incised jar, F31-8.

Documentation of Associated and Unassociated Caddo Funerary Objects

SITE NO.: 41NA49

FEATURE: 31

VESSEL NO.: F31-9

NON-PLASTICS: grog-hematite

VESSEL FORM: Bottle with a straight neck, direct rim, and rounded lip

CORE COLOR: Undetermined

INTERIOR SURFACE COLOR: dark brown (10YR 3/3)

EXTERIOR SURFACE COLOR: dark brown (10YR 3/3)

WALL THICKNESS: 5.2 mm at the neck

INTERIOR SURFACE TREATMENT: none

EXTERIOR SURFACE TREATMENT: burnished

HEIGHT: 17.5 cm

ORIFICE DIAMETER: 6.1 cm

DIAMETER AT BOTTOM OF RIM OR NECK: 5.3 cm

BASE DIAMETER: 8.3 cm

ESTIMATED VOLUME: 0.6 liters

DECORATION: This bottle has vertically-oriented engraved scrolls repeated three times around the vessel body (Figure 26). The scrolls have two parts: (a) a single curvilinear engraved line that hooks around (b) narrow cross-hatched zones that form vertical, circular, and hooked arm elements (Hart [1982:57] identifies the hooked arm element as the *Means* scroll). Within the circular cross-hatched element are two smaller circles, the innermost also being cross-hatched. Although not well-preserved, a red clay pigment appears to have been rubbed in the engraved design.

TYPE: Nacogdoches Engraved (Hart 1982: Figure 3-7c).

Figure 26. Nacogdoches Engraved bottle, F31-9.

Documentation of Associated and Unassociated Caddo Funerary Objects

SITE NO.: 41NA49

FEATURE: 31

VESSEL NO.: F31-10

NON-PLASTICS: grog

VESSEL FORM: Jar with direct rim and a rounded, exterior folded, lip; there are also four rim peaks.

CORE COLOR: Undetermined

INTERIOR SURFACE COLOR: brownish-yellow (10YR 6/6)

EXTERIOR SURFACE COLOR: brownish-yellow (10YR 6/6)

WALL THICKNESS: 7.1 mm

INTERIOR SURFACE TREATMENT: smoothed on the rim

EXTERIOR SURFACE TREATMENT: smoothed only on the vessel body; fire clouds

HEIGHT: 10.5 cm

ORIFICE DIAMETER: 13.1 cm

DIAMETER AT BOTTOM OF RIM OR NECK: 10.9 cm

BASE DIAMETER: 6.4 cm

ESTIMATED VOLUME: 0.8 liters

DECORATION: There is a row of tool punctates on the vessel lip, and the rim is horizontally brushed (Figure 27). A second row of tool punctates are at the rim-body juncture of the jar. The vessel body has eight vertically brushed panels defined by eight vertical sets of paired tool punctates; half of these double punctated rows are aligned below the four rim peaks. Within each of the brushed panels is a single row of tool punctations.

TYPE: Reavely Brushed-Incised (see Hart 1982: Figure 3-10b).

Figure 27. Reavely Brushed-Incised jar, F31-10.

Documentation of Associated and Unassociated Caddo Funerary Objects

SITE NO.: 41NA49

FEATURE: Feature 31

VESSEL NO.: F31-11

NON-PLASTICS: bone and grog; the vessel has a sandy paste

VESSEL FORM: Carinated bowl with an everted rim and a thick, rounded, exterior folded, lip

CORE COLOR: E (incompletely oxidized during firing)

INTERIOR SURFACE COLOR: light yellowish-brown (10YR 6/4)

EXTERIOR SURFACE COLOR: light yellowish-brown (10YR 6/4)

WALL THICKNESS: 4.2 mm

INTERIOR SURFACE TREATMENT: smoothed

EXTERIOR SURFACE TREATMENT: smoothed; there is a small amount of green staining visible on the rim, perhaps from contact with a copper artifact or contact with glauconitic-rich clay.

HEIGHT: 5.0 cm

ORIFICE DIAMETER: 7.7 cm

DIAMETER AT BOTTOM OF RIM OR NECK: 7.1 cm

BASE DIAMETER: 5.1 cm

ESTIMATED VOLUME: 0.15 liters

DECORATION: The rim is plain, and there is a row of small tool punctations (not rocker stamping, as Hart [1982:77] suggested) at the vessel carination point (Figure 28). The vessel body has horizontal brushing marks.

TYPE: Brushed-punctated utility ware (Hart 1982:77).

Figure 28. Brushed-punctated carinated bowl, F31-11.

Documentation of Associated and Unassociated Caddo Funerary Objects

SITE NO.: 41NA49

FEATURE: 31

VESSEL NO.: F31-12

NON-PLASTICS: grog

VESSEL FORM: Olla with a direct rim and a rounded lip (Figure 29)

CORE COLOR: Undetermined

INTERIOR SURFACE COLOR: reddish-yellow (7.5YR 6/6)

EXTERIOR SURFACE COLOR: reddish-yellow (7.5YR 6/6)

WALL THICKNESS: 5.3 mm

INTERIOR SURFACE TREATMENT: smoothed on the neck

EXTERIOR SURFACE TREATMENT: burnished

HEIGHT: 24.5 cm

ORIFICE DIAMETER: 9.2 cm

DIAMETER AT BOTTOM OF RIM OR NECK: 9.1 cm

BASE DIAMETER: 10.2 cm

ESTIMATED VOLUME: 2.0 liters

DECORATION: Plain

TYPE: Undetermined plain ware vessel (Hart 1982:87).

Figure 29. Plain olla, F31-12.

Documentation of Associated and Unassociated Caddo Funerary Objects

SITE NO.: 41NA49

FEATURE: 31

VESSEL NO.: F31-13

NON-PLASTICS: bone and charred organic materials

VESSEL FORM: Jar with an everted rim and a rounded lip (Figure 30)

CORE COLOR: Undetermined

INTERIOR SURFACE COLOR: brown (10YR 4/3) and yellowish-red (5YR 5/6)

EXTERIOR SURFACE COLOR: brown (10YR 4/3)

WALL THICKNESS: 5.6 mm

INTERIOR SURFACE TREATMENT: smoothed

EXTERIOR SURFACE TREATMENT: smoothed, but with a pitted surface caused by the leaching of the bone temper

HEIGHT: 10.0 cm

ORIFICE DIAMETER: 11.9 cm

DIAMETER AT BOTTOM OF RIM OR NECK: 10.1 cm

BASE DIAMETER: 5.8 cm

ESTIMATED VOLUME: 0.7 liters

DECORATION: Plain (Hart 1982:86)

TYPE: Undetermined plain ware vessel

Figure 30. Plain jar, F31-13.

SITE NO.: 41NA49

FEATURE: 31

VESSEL NO.: F31-14

NON-PLASTICS: grog

VESSEL FORM: Jar with a direct to slightly everted rim and a rounded lip

CORE COLOR: A (fired and cooled in an oxidizing environment)

INTERIOR SURFACE COLOR: light brown (7.5YR 6/3)

EXTERIOR SURFACE COLOR: gray (7.5YR 6/1), and very dark gray (10YR 3/1) fire clouds

WALL THICKNESS: 7.6 mm

INTERIOR SURFACE TREATMENT: smoothed on rim only

EXTERIOR SURFACE TREATMENT: smoothed on rim; fire clouding

HEIGHT: 13.6 cm

ORIFICE DIAMETER: 8.7 cm

DIAMETER AT BOTTOM OF RIM OR NECK: 8.1 cm

BASE DIAMETER: 3.7 cm

ESTIMATED VOLUME: 0.8 liters

DECORATION: The rim is plain, but the vessel body is covered with irregular rows of tool punctations from the rim-body juncture to near the flat base (Figure 31).

TYPE: Undetermined punctated utility ware vessel (Hart 1982:87); it is incorrectly listed as Feature 95, Vessel 14 in Hart (1982:87).

Figure 31. Punctated jar from Feature 31, F31-14.

Documentation of Associated and Unassociated Caddo Funerary Objects

SITE NO.: 41NA49

FEATURE: 31

VESSEL NO.: F31-15

NON-PLASTICS: grog

VESSEL FORM: simple bowl with a direct rim and a rounded lip; the vessel has rim tabs, and is probably an effigy vessel (Suhm and Jelks 1962:47), but the effigy head is broken off and missing (Figure 32). The effigy head was not found in Feature 31, and "presumably broken off prior to the placement of this vessel in the burial" (Hart 1982:76).

CORE COLOR: F (fired in a reducing environment, but cooled in the open air)

INTERIOR SURFACE COLOR: brown (7.5YR 4/4)

EXTERIOR SURFACE COLOR: brown (10YR 4/3)

WALL THICKNESS: 5.4 mm

INTERIOR SURFACE TREATMENT: smoothed on the upper rim and on the rim tabs

EXTERIOR SURFACE TREATMENT: smoothed

HEIGHT: 7.0 cm

ORIFICE DIAMETER: 12.6 cm

DIAMETER AT BOTTOM OF RIM OR NECK: N/A

BASE DIAMETER: 6.3 cm

ESTIMATED VOLUME: 0.35 liters

DECORATION: There are three broad horizontal incised lines on the rim

TYPE: Undetermined incised effigy vessel (Hart 1982:76).

Figure 32a. Incised effigy vessel from Feature 31, Vessel F31-15, side view.

Figure 32b. Incised effigy vessel from Feature 31, Vessel F31-15, top view.

SITE NO.: 41NA49

FEATURE: 95

VESSEL NO.: F95-1

NON-PLASTICS: bone, hematite, and grog

VESSEL FORM: Carinated bowl with a direct rim and a rounded, exterior folded lip

CORE COLOR: F (fired in a reducing environment, but cooled in the open air)

INTERIOR SURFACE COLOR: yellowish-red (5YR 5/6)

EXTERIOR SURFACE COLOR: yellowish-red (5YR 5/6)

WALL THICKNESS: 6.6 mm on the rim; 8.4 mm on the body; and 9.1 mm on the base

INTERIOR SURFACE TREATMENT: smoothed on the rim

EXTERIOR SURFACE TREATMENT: smoothed on the rim

HEIGHT: 16.8 cm

ORIFICE DIAMETER: 28.5 cm

DIAMETER AT BOTTOM OF RIM OR NECK: 26.0 cm

BASE DIAMETER: 8.7 cm

ESTIMATED VOLUME: 4.4 liters

DECORATION: The rim has an engraved circle and scroll motif that is repeated five times around the vessel (Figure 33). The scrolls are separated from each other by multiple sets of engraved diagonal lines

TYPE: Nacogdoches Engraved (Hart 1982: Figure 3-5c).

Figure 33. Nacogdoches Engraved carinated bowl, F95-1.

Documentation of Associated and Unassociated Caddo Funerary Objects

SITE NO.: 41NA49

FEATURE: 95

VESSEL NO.: F95-2/F95-5 (field notes indicate that sherds with these two designations are part of the same fragmentary vessel)

NON-PLASTICS: grog and hematite; the vessel has a sandy paste

VESSEL FORM: Jar with a direct rim and a rounded lip

CORE COLOR: F (fired in a reducing environment, but cooled in the open air)

INTERIOR SURFACE COLOR: strong brown (7.5YR 5/6)

EXTERIOR SURFACE COLOR: yellowish-brown (10YR 5/4) to black (10YR 2/1)

WALL THICKNESS: 5.6 mm; the base is 17.2 mm thick

INTERIOR SURFACE TREATMENT: smoothed

EXTERIOR SURFACE TREATMENT: smoothed

HEIGHT: Undetermined

ORIFICE DIAMETER: Undetermined

DIAMETER AT BOTTOM OF RIM OR NECK: Undetermined

BASE DIAMETER: 9.0 cm

ESTIMATED VOLUME: Undetermined

DECORATION: There is a horizontal band of tool punctates on the rim, and pendant from the lowermost row is a circular row of tool punctates (Figure 34a). The body of the vessel is plain (Figure 34b).

TYPE: Undetermined punctated utility ware vessel (Hart 1982:87-88).

Figure 34a. Punctated vessel fragment from Feature 95, F95-2, rim sherds.

Figure 34b. Punctated vessel fragment from Feature 95, F95-2, body and base sherds.

Documentation of Associated and Unassociated Caddo Funerary Objects

SITE NO.: 41NA49

FEATURE: 95

VESSEL NO.: F95-3

NON-PLASTICS: grog

VESSEL FORM: Carinated bowl with a direct rim and a flat lip

CORE COLOR: E (incompletely oxidized during firing)

INTERIOR SURFACE COLOR: light reddish-brown (5YR 6/4)

EXTERIOR SURFACE COLOR: brown (10YR 5/3) to dark brown (10YR 3/3)

WALL THICKNESS: 8.0 mm

INTERIOR SURFACE TREATMENT: burnished

EXTERIOR SURFACE TREATMENT: burnished

HEIGHT: 7.5 cm

ORIFICE DIAMETER: 14.5 cm

DIAMETER AT BOTTOM OF RIM OR NECK: 13.4 cm

BASE DIAMETER: 7.5 cm

ESTIMATED VOLUME: 0.7 liters

DECORATION: There are five different and distinct, but poorly executed, engraved modes around the vessel rim, beginning with a semi-circle inside a larger semi-circle; there are excised triangular spurs on the outer semi-circle (Figure 35). The second mode is a rectangle with triangular excised corners (resembling *Mode A* engraving, see Hart [1982:82]), while the third has a set of two semi-circular lines with irregular excised areas. The fourth mode is a set of four semi-circles, and the last is a set of two semi-circles.

TYPE: Undetermined Engraved (Hart 1982:Figure 3-14d).

Figure 35. Undetermined engraved carinated bowl, F95-3.

Documentation of Associated and Unassociated Caddo Funerary Objects

SITE NO.: 41NA49

FEATURE: 95

VESSEL NO.: F95-4

NON-PLASTICS: grog

VESSEL FORM: Jar with a direct to slightly everted rim and a rounded, exterior folded, lip

CORE COLOR: F (fired in a reducing environment but cooled in the open air)

INTERIOR SURFACE COLOR: yellowish-red (5YR 5/8)

EXTERIOR SURFACE COLOR: dark reddish-brown (5YR 3/2)

WALL THICKNESS: 5.5 mm on the rim; 4.6 mm on the body; and 5.9 mm on the base

INTERIOR SURFACE TREATMENT: smoothed on the rim and base; burnished on the body

EXTERIOR SURFACE TREATMENT: none

HEIGHT: 15.4 cm

ORIFICE DIAMETER: 16.5 cm

DIAMETER AT BOTTOM OF RIM OR NECK: 12.0 cm

BASE DIAMETER: 8.1 cm

ESTIMATED VOLUME: 1.5 liters

DECORATION: There is a punctated row on the lip. The rim is horizontally brushed, with a row of linear punctates midway on the rim, and a second row of linear punctates at the rim-body juncture (Figure 36). The body has a complicated brushed, punctated, and appliqued design composed of alternating appliqued semi-circles (each composed of two appliqued fillet semi-circles) that is repeated twice. The space between the appliqued fillet semi-circles is filled with vertical and curvilinear brushing marks, a single row of tool punctates between the inner and outer semi-circles, and there is a short vertical appliqued fillet inside the inner appliqued fillet semi-circle (see Figure 36).

TYPE: Reavely Brushed-Incised (Hart 1982: Figure 3-11a).

Figure 36. Reavely Brushed-Incised jar, F95-4.

SITE NO.: 41NA49

FEATURE: 95

VESSEL NO.: F95-6

NON-PLASTICS: bone

VESSEL FORM: Bowl with a direct rim and a broad, flat, lip (Figure 37a); the rim is a Redwine mode pie-crust form with 16 scallops (Figure 37b)

CORE COLOR: B (fired and cooled in a reducing environment)

INTERIOR SURFACE COLOR: very dark gray (10YR 3/1)

EXTERIOR SURFACE COLOR: pale brown (10YR 6/3)

WALL THICKNESS: 8.4 mm

INTERIOR SURFACE TREATMENT: burnished

EXTERIOR SURFACE TREATMENT: burnished, but eroded

HEIGHT: 5.0 cm

ORIFICE DIAMETER: 15.5 cm

DIAMETER AT BOTTOM OF RIM OR NECK: N/A

BASE DIAMETER: 10.4 cm

ESTIMATED VOLUME: 0.3 liters

DECORATION: The rim has an engraved motif (labeled *Mode A engraved* by Hart [1982:78 and Figure 3-13a]) repeated four times around the vessel; each repeated motif is separated from the other by one or two vertical engraved lines. The engraved motif consists of squares with triangular-shaped hatched corners and a small engraved circle in the center of the square. Three of the small circles are filled with cross-hatched lines, but one has vertical engraved lines within it (Figure 37a).

TYPE: Undetermined Engraved (Hart 1982:Figure 3-13b), but closely resembles examples of Poynor Engraved (cf. Suhm and Jelks 1962).

Figure 37a. Vessel F95-6, side view.

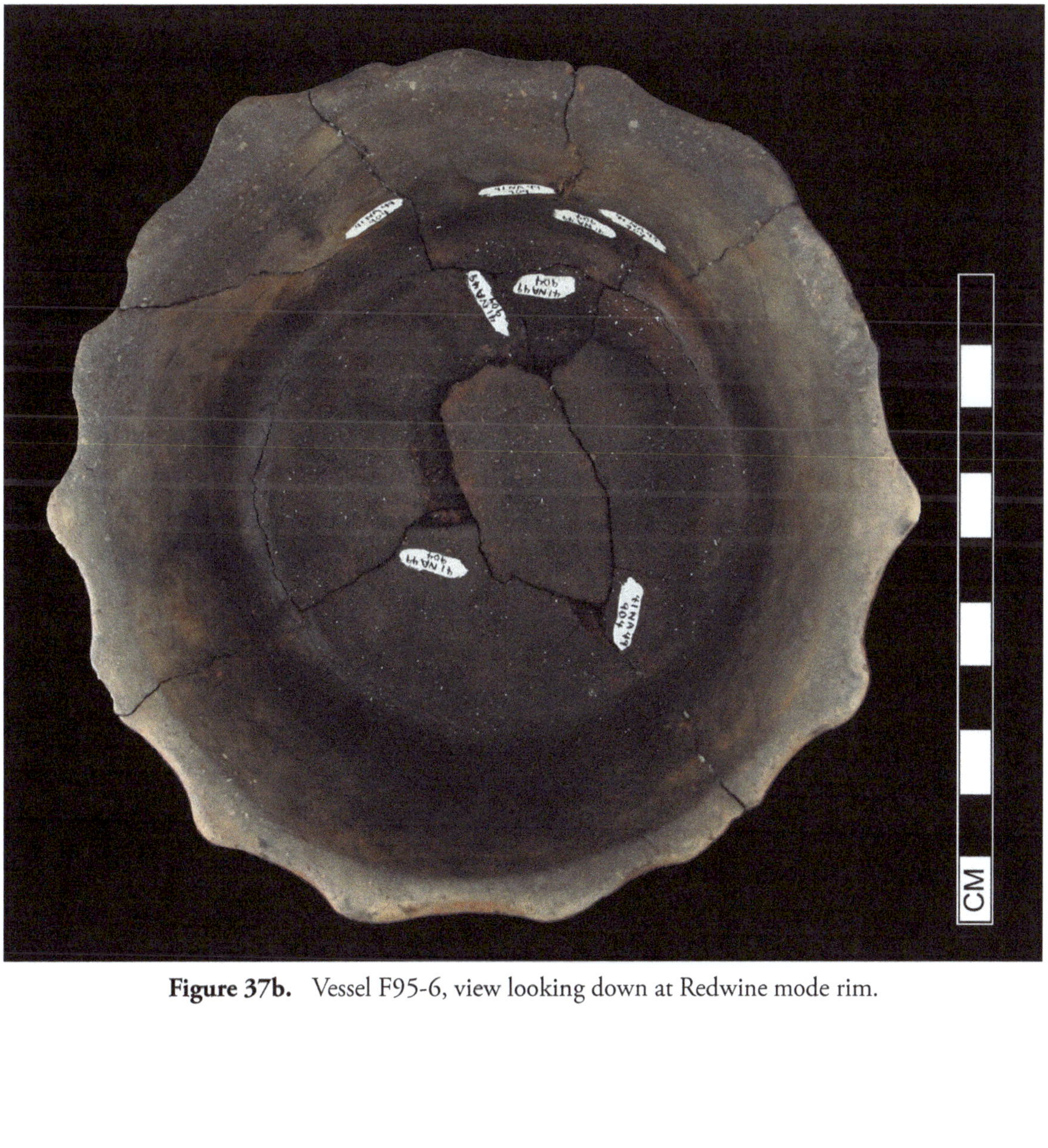

Figure 37b. Vessel F95-6, view looking down at Redwine mode rim.

95

Documentation of Associated and Unassociated Caddo Funerary Objects

SITE NO.: 41NA49

FEATURE: 95

VESSEL NO.: F95-7

NON-PLASTICS: bone

VESSEL FORM: carinated bowl with a direct rim and a rounded, exterior folded, lip

CORE COLOR: F (fired in a reducing environment, but cooled in the open air)

INTERIOR SURFACE COLOR: yellowish-red (5YR 4/6)

EXTERIOR SURFACE COLOR: reddish-brown (5YR 4/4); possible patches of a black slip (Hart 1982:56)

WALL THICKNESS: 6.2 mm

INTERIOR SURFACE TREATMENT: burnished

EXTERIOR SURFACE TREATMENT: burnished

HEIGHT: 12.0 cm

ORIFICE DIAMETER: 24.4 cm

DIAMETER AT BOTTOM OF RIM OR NECK: 21.5 cm

BASE DIAMETER: 9.3 cm

ESTIMATED VOLUME: 1.8 liters

DECORATION: There is an engraved scroll and circle motif repeated seven times around the vessel rim (Figure 38). The *Crockett* scrolls and scroll dividers are composed of narrow cross-hatched bands, while the central circle element has three circular lines; the innermost has crossed vertical and horizontal lines (forming a cross), with small hatched and alternating triangular areas pendant from the intersecting straight lines. A red clay pigment has been rubbed in the engraved lines.

TYPE: Nacogdoches Engraved (Hart 1982: Figure 3-7b).

Figure 38. Nacogdoches Engraved carinated bowl, F95-7.

Documentation of Associated and Unassociated Caddo Funerary Objects

SITE NO.: 41NA49

FEATURE: 95

VESSEL NO.: F95-8

NON-PLASTICS: grog and hematite

VESSEL FORM: Compound bowl with a direct rim and a rounded, exterior folded, lip

CORE COLOR: F (fired in a reducing environment, but cooled in the open air)

INTERIOR SURFACE COLOR: light yellowish-brown (10YR 6/4); fire clouds on base and lower body

EXTERIOR SURFACE COLOR: light yellowish-brown (10YR 6/4); fire clouds on the lower rim panel; organic residue on the lower rim panel and upper body; possible remnants of a black slip (Hart 1982:51)

WALL THICKNESS: 4.6 mm

INTERIOR SURFACE TREATMENT: burnished on the short upper rim panel; smoothed on the lower rim panel

EXTERIOR SURFACE TREATMENT: burnished, but eroded

HEIGHT: 12.5 cm

ORIFICE DIAMETER: 19.9 cm

DIAMETER AT BOTTOM OF RIM OR NECK: 16.8 cm

BASE DIAMETER: 8.3 cm

ESTIMATED VOLUME: 2.0 liters

DECORATION: The upper rim panel has three horizontal engraved lines (Figure 39). The lower panel has an engraved scroll motif that is repeated four times around the vessel. This consists of large semi-circular elements with three narrow cross-hatched zones within it (including a triangular hatched area in one corner of the semi-circle and two opposed diagonal cross-hatched zones), and a single cross-hatched circle on or intersecting the semi-circular line.

TYPE: Nacogdoches Engraved (Hart 1982: Figure 3-6a).

Figure 39. Nacogdoches Engraved compound bowl, F95-8.

Documentation of Associated and Unassociated Caddo Funerary Objects

SITE NO.: 41NA49

FEATURE: 95

VESSEL NO.: F95-9

NON-PLASTICS: grog, with a sandy paste

VESSEL FORM: Jar with a direct rim and a flat lip

CORE COLOR: F (fired in a reducing environment but cooled in the open air)

INTERIOR SURFACE COLOR: very dark gray (5YR 3/1) on the rim and yellowish-red (5YR 4/6) on the body

EXTERIOR SURFACE COLOR: brown (7.5YR 5/4)

WALL THICKNESS: 5.9 mm on the rim, 6.3 mm on the body, and 6.7 mm on the base

INTERIOR SURFACE TREATMENT: none

EXTERIOR SURFACE TREATMENT: none

HEIGHT: 10.2 cm

ORIFICE DIAMETER: 14.5 cm

DIAMETER AT BOTTOM OF RIM OR NECK: 12.6 cm

BASE DIAMETER: Undetermined

ESTIMATED VOLUME: 0.9 liters

DECORATION: The rim has two rows of tool punctates, one under the lip and the other at the rim-body juncture; the area between the punctates has light horizontal brushing marks. The vessel body has diagonal brushing (Figure 40).

TYPE: Undetermined brushed-punctated utility ware vessel (Hart 1982:77).

Figure 40. Brushed-punctated jar, F95-9.

Documentation of Associated and Unassociated Caddo Funerary Objects

SITE NO.: 41NA49

FEATURE: 95

VESSEL NO.: F95-10

NON-PLASTICS: grog-hematite

VESSEL FORM: Bowl with a direct rim and a rounded, slightly rolled, lip

CORE COLOR: F (fired in a reducing environment, but cooled in the open air)

INTERIOR SURFACE COLOR: strong brown (7.5YR 5/8)

EXTERIOR SURFACE COLOR: brown (7.5YR 4/4)

WALL THICKNESS: 8.4 mm

INTERIOR SURFACE TREATMENT: burnished

EXTERIOR SURFACE TREATMENT: burnished

HEIGHT: 7.8 cm

ORIFICE DIAMETER: 13.6 cm

DIAMETER AT BOTTOM OF RIM OR NECK: 7.8 cm

BASE DIAMETER: 7.2 cm

ESTIMATED VOLUME: 0.4 liters

DECORATION: The rim has five repeated vertical scrolls (Hart [1982] refers to it as a *Means* scroll) composed of two or three curvilinear engraved lines that hook around a fourth curvilinear line. The area between the hooked curvilinear lines on three of the scrolls has a small circle with five ticked lines or rays (Figure 41).

TYPE: Nacogdoches Engraved (Hart 1982: Figure 3-8d).

Figure 41. Nacogdoches Engraved bowl, F95-10.

Documentation of Associated and Unassociated Caddo Funerary Objects

SITE NO.: 41NA49

FEATURE: 95

VESSEL NO.: F95-11

NON-PLASTICS: grog and hematite

VESSEL FORM: Carinated bowl with a direct rim and a rounded, exterior folded lip

CORE COLOR: F

INTERIOR SURFACE COLOR: reddish-brown (5YR 4/4)

EXTERIOR SURFACE COLOR: brown (7.5YR 4/4)

WALL THICKNESS: 10.5 cm

INTERIOR SURFACE TREATMENT: smoothed on the upper part of the rim

EXTERIOR SURFACE TREATMENT: smoothed; fire clouding

HEIGHT: 10.5 cm

ORIFICE DIAMETER: 22.5 cm

DIAMETER AT BOTTOM OF RIM OR NECK: 16.5 cm

BASE DIAMETER: 11.5 cm

ESTIMATED VOLUME: 1.4 liters

DECORATION: The rim has 12 repeating incised triangles filled with tool punctations. The triangles alternate along the rim, with either their apex at the rim or at the carination (Figure 42).

TYPE: Undetermined incised-punctated utility ware vessel (Hart 1982:93 and Figure 3-16b), with a broad similarity to Pennington Punctated-Incised vessels (Suhm and Jelks 1962:Plate 61j).

Figure 42. Incised-punctated carinated bowl, F95-11.

SITE NO.: 41NA49

FEATURE: 95

VESSEL NO.: F95-12

NON-PLASTICS: bone-hematite

VESSEL FORM: Compound bowl with a direct rim and a rounded, exterior folded lip

CORE COLOR: F (fired in a reducing environment, but cooled in the open air)

INTERIOR SURFACE COLOR: dark grayish-brown (10YR 4/2) on the rim and pale brown (10YR 6/3) on the body

EXTERIOR SURFACE COLOR: dark grayish-brown (10YR 4/2); fire clouding on the base

WALL THICKNESS: 5.7 mm on the rim and 6.2 mm on the body

INTERIOR SURFACE TREATMENT: burnished

EXTERIOR SURFACE TREATMENT: burnished, but eroded on the lower body

HEIGHT: 8.0 cm

ORIFICE DIAMETER: 16.3 cm

DIAMETER AT BOTTOM OF RIM OR NECK: 13.2 cm

BASE DIAMETER: 8.5 cm

ESTIMATED VOLUME: 1.0 liters

DECORATION: The upper panel has 15 repeating sets of four curvilinear vertical engraved lines. The lower panel has 17 sets of hatched triangles, each set comprised of triangles pendant from the upper part of the lower panel, with their apex between along the panel mid-line (Figure 43). The two panels are separated by horizontal engraved lines.

TYPE: Undetermined Engraved (Hart 1982: Figure 3-14c).

Figure 43. Undetermined engraved compound bowl, F95-12.

Documentation of Associated and Unassociated Caddo Funerary Objects

SITE NO.: 41NA49

FEATURE: 95   VESSEL NO.: F95-13

NON-PLASTICS: grog, bone, and hematite

VESSEL FORM: Jar with a direct but exterior thickened rim and a flat lip

CORE COLOR: G (fired in a reducing environment, but cooled in the open air)

INTERIOR SURFACE COLOR: very dark grayish-brown (10YR 3/2) on the rim and dark yellowish-brown (10YR 4/4) on the body

EXTERIOR SURFACE COLOR: dark yellowish-brown (10YR 4/4)

WALL THICKNESS: 6.5 mm on the rim and body and 9.5 mm on the base

INTERIOR SURFACE TREATMENT: smoothed on the rim; interior organic residue on the rim and upper body

EXTERIOR SURFACE TREATMENT: poorly smoothed on the rim

HEIGHT: 13.0 cm   ORIFICE DIAMETER: 17.0 cm

DIAMETER AT BOTTOM OF RIM OR NECK: 14.5 cm

BASE DIAMETER: 9.0 cm   ESTIMATED VOLUME: 1.3 liters

DECORATION: The vessel has an incised-punctated decoration on both the rim and body (Figure 44). The rim decoration consists of horizontal incised interlocking scrolls (filled with punctates) repeated three times with attached and stacked hour glass-shaped incised zones filled with punctates. Each scroll is divided by a large incised-punctated hour glass-shaped zone that extends from the top to the bottom of the rim. There are single rows of diagonal tool punctates under the lip and at the rim-body juncture.

    The incised-punctated body decoration includes stacked incised diamonds (four in total) or parallelograms divided by two sets of opposed diagonal incised and vertical incised lines (see Figure 44). Two of the stacked incised diamonds have negative diamond-shaped areas outlined by a zone of tool punctations, while the other two have smaller diamond-shaped incised areas within the larger stacked incised diamonds. Both have tool punctations within the incised zones, randomly placed within the larger stacked diamonds and in two short central rows within the smaller diamonds.

TYPE: Washington Square Paneled (Hart 1982: Figure 3-12d).

Figure 44. Washington Square Paneled jar, F95-13.

Documentation of Associated and Unassociated Caddo Funerary Objects

SITE NO.: 41NA49

FEATURE: 95

VESSEL NO.: F95-14

NON-PLASTICS: grog

VESSEL FORM: Compound or shouldered bowl with an everted rim and a rounded, exterior folded, lip

CORE COLOR: B (fired and cooled in a reducing environment)

INTERIOR SURFACE COLOR: yellowish-brown (10YR 5/4)

EXTERIOR SURFACE COLOR: pale brown (10YR 6/3) to very dark gray (10YR 3/1)

WALL THICKNESS: 6.1 mm

INTERIOR SURFACE TREATMENT: burnished

EXTERIOR SURFACE TREATMENT: burnished

HEIGHT: 8.5 cm

ORIFICE DIAMETER: 18.0 cm

DIAMETER AT BOTTOM OF RIM OR NECK: 16.5 cm

BASE DIAMETER: 8.0 cm

ESTIMATED VOLUME: 1.2 liters

DECORATION: The upper rim panel is plain, but the lower panel has engraved scrolls repeated six times around the vessel (Figure 45). Each scroll motif has a central curvilinear line with hatched zones both above and below this line. The scrolls are divided by small negative engraved boxes (with the boxes outlined by a hatched zone), six in number, filled with a single short vertical engraved line.

TYPE: Undetermined Engraved (Hart 1982: Figure 3-14a). Hart (1982:81) mistakenly labels this as vessel F95-26.

Figure 45. Undetermined engraved compound bowl, F95-14.

Documentation of Associated and Unassociated Caddo Funerary Objects

SITE NO.: 41NA49

FEATURE: 95

VESSEL NO.: F95-15

NON-PLASTICS: grog, bone, and hematite

VESSEL FORM: Carinated bowl with a direct to slightly everted rim and a rounded, exterior folded lip

CORE COLOR: F (fired in a reducing environment but cooled in the open air)

INTERIOR SURFACE COLOR: brownish-yellow (10YR 6/6), with fire clouding on rim

EXTERIOR SURFACE COLOR: brownish-yellow (10YR 6/6)

WALL THICKNESS: 6.9 mm

INTERIOR SURFACE TREATMENT: burnished on the rim, smoothed on the body

EXTERIOR SURFACE TREATMENT: burnished; pitted and eroded on the vessel body

HEIGHT: 9.5 cm

ORIFICE DIAMETER: 15.7 cm

DIAMETER AT BOTTOM OF RIM OR NECK: 13.4 cm

BASE DIAMETER: 7.6 cm

ESTIMATED VOLUME: 0.9 liters

DECORATION: The rim of the vessel has an engraved-fine rocker stamped decoration within a panel defined by upper and lower horizontal engraved lines. There are 19 downward-pointing hatched triangles pendant from the upper horizontal engraved line, as well as a horizontal-vertical rocker stamped scroll (Figure 46). The lower part of the rocker stamped scroll forms three boxes that enclose narrow cross-hatched zones with either two curvilinear hooks or two curvilinear hooks and a cross-hatched semi-circle or arc.

TYPE: Undetermined engraved-rocker stamped fine ware vessel (Hart 1982:88 and Figure 3-15b).

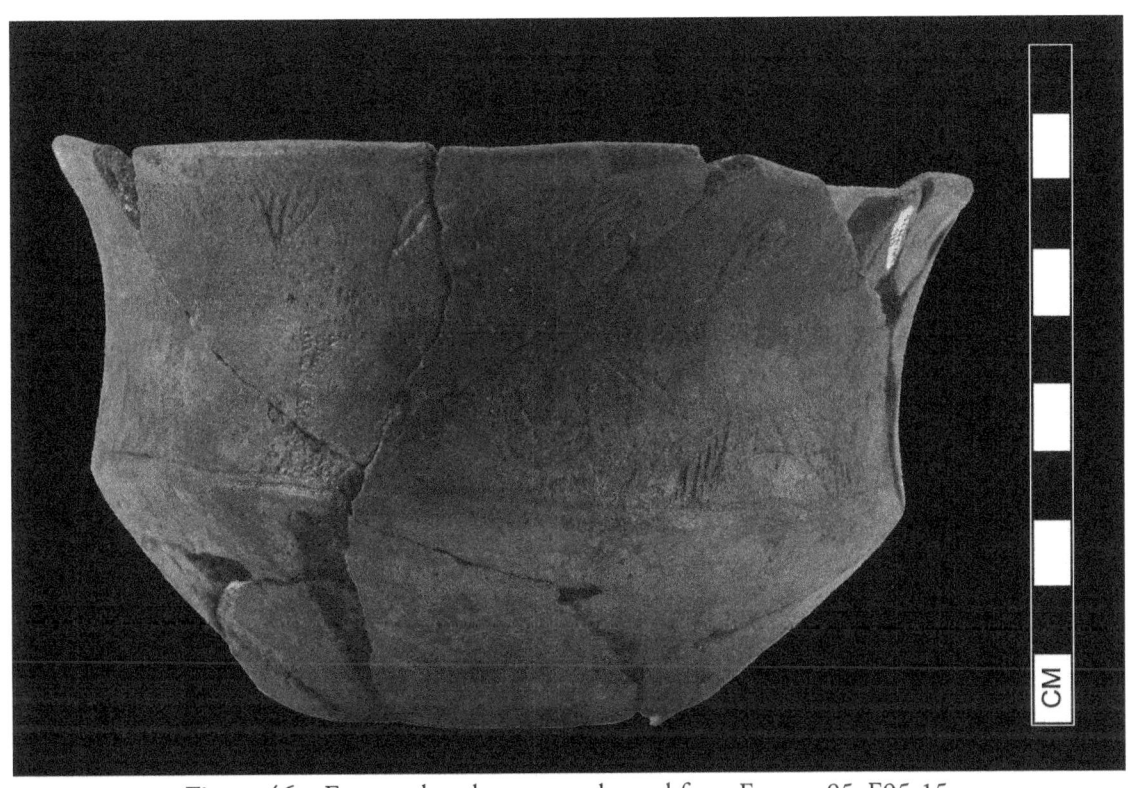

Figure 46. Engraved-rocker stamped vessel from Feature 95, F95-15.

Documentation of Associated and Unassociated Caddo Funerary Objects

SITE NO.: 41NA49

FEATURE: 95

VESSEL NO.: F95-16

NON-PLASTICS: grog-bone

VESSEL FORM: Compound bowl with a direct rim and a rounded, exterior folded, lip

CORE COLOR: F (fired in a reducing environment and cooled in the open air)

INTERIOR SURFACE COLOR: yellowish-red (5YR 5/6)

EXTERIOR SURFACE COLOR: dark reddish-gray (5YR 4/2) to yellowish-red (5YR 5/6)

WALL THICKNESS: 6.2 mm

INTERIOR SURFACE TREATMENT: burnished

EXTERIOR SURFACE TREATMENT: burnished

HEIGHT: Undetermined

ORIFICE DIAMETER: Undetermined

DIAMETER AT BOTTOM OF RIM OR NECK: Undetermined

BASE DIAMETER: 7.8 cm

ESTIMATED VOLUME: Undetermined

DECORATION: The upper rim panel has a single horizontal engraved line, while the lower panel has a cross-hatched semi-circular scroll motif repeated four times around the vessel (Figure 47). Within each of these central semi-circles is a small circle defined by a single engraved line. The fill zones above and below the scrolls are composed of four hatched triangles. A kaolin clay pigment has been rubbed in the engraved lines.

TYPE: Nacogdoches Engraved (Hart 1982: Figure 3-7a).

Figure 47. Nacogdoches Engraved compound bowl, F95-16.

Documentation of Associated and Unassociated Caddo Funerary Objects

SITE NO.: 41NA49

FEATURE: 95

VESSEL NO.: F95-17

NON-PLASTICS: grog

VESSEL FORM: Globular or compound bowl with an everted rim and a flat, exterior folded, lip

CORE COLOR: F (fired in a reducing environment, but cooled in the open air)

INTERIOR SURFACE COLOR: yellowish-brown (10YR 5/6)

EXTERIOR SURFACE COLOR: yellowish-red (5YR 5/6)

WALL THICKNESS: 6.3 mm; the base is 9.8 mm thick

INTERIOR SURFACE TREATMENT: roughened

EXTERIOR SURFACE TREATMENT: smoothed

HEIGHT: 8.5 cm

ORIFICE DIAMETER: 13.5 cm

DIAMETER AT BOTTOM OF RIM OR NECK: 12.5 cm

BASE DIAMETER: 6.5 cm

ESTIMATED VOLUME: 0.5 liters

DECORATION: The vessel has a poorly executed engraved design on the lower rim panel, consisting of crude scrolls and elements with concentric circles, defined at the top and bottom by horizontal engraved lines (Figure 48).

TYPE: Undetermined engraved fine ware vessel (Hart 1982:84). Hart (1982:84) further suggests that the color and paste of this vessel is distinctly different from other Washington Square Mound site vessels, and notes a similarity to Caddo ceramic vessels found in the upper Neches River basin in Anderson and Cherokee counties, Texas.

Figure 48. Undetermined engraved compound bowl, F95-17.

Documentation of Associated and Unassociated Caddo Funerary Objects

SITE NO.: 41NA49

FEATURE: 95

VESSEL NO.: F95-18

NON-PLASTICS: grog and hematite

VESSEL FORM: oval-shaped bowl with a direct rim and a rounded, exterior folded lip

CORE COLOR: A (fired and cooled in an oxidizing environment)

INTERIOR SURFACE COLOR: strong brown (7.5YR 5/6)

EXTERIOR SURFACE COLOR: light brown (7.5YR 6/4)

WALL THICKNESS: 7.2 mm

INTERIOR SURFACE TREATMENT: smoothed on the upper rim; the base is eroded and pitted

EXTERIOR SURFACE TREATMENT: smoothed to poorly burnished

HEIGHT: 7.5 cm

ORIFICE DIAMETER: 15.3 cm to 18.2 cm

DIAMETER AT BOTTOM OF RIM OR NECK: N/A

BASE DIAMETER: 8.5-10.2 cm

ESTIMATED VOLUME: 0.55 liters

DECORATION: The upper part of the uniquely-shaped vessel has an engraved continuous scroll motif (a *Crockett* scroll) repeated three times around the rim (Figure 49). The central part of each scroll is a circle. In one case, one of the scroll lines is a narrow cross-hatched zone rather than a 1-2 closely-spaced lines.

TYPE: Nacogdoches Engraved (Hart 1982: Figure 3-6b).

Figure 49. Nacogdoches Engraved bowl, F95-18.

Documentation of Associated and Unassociated Caddo Funerary Objects

SITE NO.: 41NA49

FEATURE: 95

VESSEL NO.: F95-19

NON-PLASTICS: grog

VESSEL FORM: Carinated bowl with a direct rim and a rounded lip

CORE COLOR: Undetermined

INTERIOR SURFACE COLOR: dark brown (7.5YR 3/4)

EXTERIOR SURFACE COLOR: very dark brown (7.5YR 3/2)

WALL THICKNESS: 6.7 mm

INTERIOR SURFACE TREATMENT: burnished

EXTERIOR SURFACE TREATMENT: burnished

HEIGHT: 11.0 cm

ORIFICE DIAMETER: 25.5 cm

DIAMETER AT BOTTOM OF RIM OR NECK: 21.5 cm

BASE DIAMETER: 9.5 cm

ESTIMATED VOLUME: 1.7 liters

DECORATION: The rim has an engraved motif (*Mode A*) repeated five times around the vessel. The motif includes five panels (defined by a vertical engraved lines and sets of pendant hatched triangles) with either one (two panels), two (two panels), or three (one panel) curvilinear and hooked scrolls within the panels (Figure 50a-b).

TYPE: Undetermined engraved fine ware vessel (Hart 1982: Figure 3-13c). It is possible that poorly preserved sherds in Lot 922 (labeled as F95-24, which it is not, see below) also are part of this vessel, based on the spiral engraved design on these sherds and June 26, 1981 (p. 23 of 32) and June 30, 1981 (p. 31) field notes on file at SFA.

Figure 50a. Undetermined engraved carinated bowl, F95-19.

Figure 50b. Undetermined engraved carinated bowl, F95-19.

SITE NO.: 41NA49

FEATURE: 95

VESSEL NO.: F95-20

NON-PLASTICS: grog and a sandy paste

VESSEL FORM: Jar with an everted rim, four rim peaks, and a rounded lip

CORE COLOR: E

INTERIOR SURFACE COLOR: brown (10YR 4/3)

EXTERIOR SURFACE COLOR: brown (10YR 4/3)

WALL THICKNESS: 6.8 mm

INTERIOR SURFACE TREATMENT: smoothed

EXTERIOR SURFACE TREATMENT: none

HEIGHT: Undetermined

ORIFICE DIAMETER: 11.6 cm

DIAMETER AT BOTTOM OF RIM OR NECK: 9.1 cm

BASE DIAMETER: Undetermined

ESTIMATED VOLUME: Undetermined

DECORATION: The rim has rows of tool punctates under the lip and at the rim-body juncture. The remainder of the rim has vertical brushing marks (Figure 51). The body is divided into panels by vertical appliqued fillets and a single horizontal row of tool punctations placed mid-way down the vessel body. The panels created by the intersecting punctated and appliqued fillets are filled with either horizontal or vertical brushing.

TYPE: Reavely Brushed-Incised (Hart 1982: Figure 3-11b).

Figure 51. Reavely Brushed-Incised jar, F95-20.

SITE NO.: 41NA49

FEATURE: 95

VESSEL NO.: F95-21

NON-PLASTICS: grog

VESSEL FORM: Carinated bowl with a direct rim and a scalloped lip (Figure 52a-b)

CORE COLOR: Undetermined

INTERIOR SURFACE COLOR: yellowish-red (5YR 4/6)

EXTERIOR SURFACE COLOR: very dark gray (7.5YR 3/1)

WALL THICKNESS: 8.1 mm

INTERIOR SURFACE TREATMENT: burnished; charred organic residue on the base

EXTERIOR SURFACE TREATMENT: burnished

HEIGHT: 8.0 cm

ORIFICE DIAMETER: 19.5 cm

DIAMETER AT BOTTOM OF RIM OR NECK: 16.0 cm

BASE DIAMETER: 9.0 cm

ESTIMATED VOLUME: 0.9 liters

DECORATION: There are panels of tool punctates repeated four times around the rim. These panels include two closely-spaced sets of four rows of four tool punctations that are connected by three longer rows of more widely-spaced punctations (with eight punctations apiece) between them (see Figure 52a).

TYPE: Washington Square Paneled (Figure 3-12a).

Figure 52a. Washington Square Paneled carinated bowl, side view.

Figure 52b. Washington Square Paneled carinated bowl, view of scalloped lip.

Documentation of Associated and Unassociated Caddo Funerary Objects

SITE NO.: 41NA49

FEATURE: 95

VESSEL NO.: F95-22

NON-PLASTICS: grog

VESSEL FORM: Carinated bowl with a direct Redwine mode pie-crust rim and a flat lip (Figure 53a-b)

CORE COLOR: B (fired and cooled in a reducing environment)

INTERIOR SURFACE COLOR: dark grayish-brown (10YR 4/2) to black (10YR 2/1)

EXTERIOR SURFACE COLOR: very dark grayish-brown (10YR 3/2)

WALL THICKNESS: 5.6 mm

INTERIOR SURFACE TREATMENT: burnished

EXTERIOR SURFACE TREATMENT: burnished

HEIGHT: 6.0 cm

ORIFICE DIAMETER: 15.0 cm

DIAMETER AT BOTTOM OF RIM OR NECK: 12.6 cm

BASE DIAMETER: 6.9 cm

ESTIMATED VOLUME: 0.55 liters

DECORATION: Engraved rectilinear and continuous scrolls repeated six times around the vessel rim (see Figure 53a). Fill zones above and below each of the scrolls are composed of hatched areas and negative ovals, one in each fill zone. The scrolls are divided by narrow vertical cross-hatched zones, except in one instance where the vertical hatched zone was not executed.

TYPE: Undetermined engraved fine ware vessel (Hart 1982: Figure 3-14b).

Figure 53a. Undetermined engraved carinated bowl, F95-22, side view.

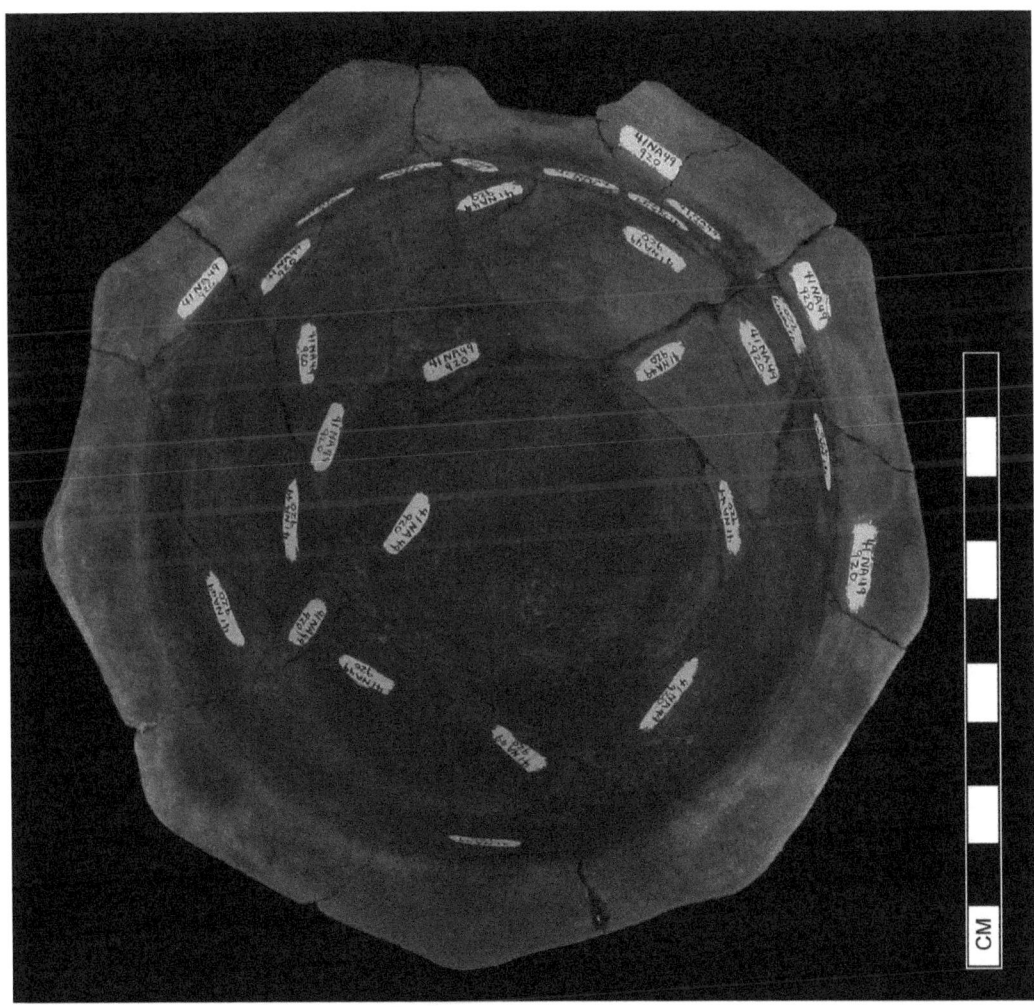

Figure 53b. Undetermined engraved carinated bowl, F95-22, view of Redwine mode rim.

Documentation of Associated and Unassociated Caddo Funerary Objects

SITE NO.: 41NA49   FEATURE: 95

VESSEL NO.: F95-23   NON-PLASTICS: grog

VESSEL FORM: Bottle with a globular body, a straight neck, and a direct rim and rounded lip

CORE COLOR: B (fired and cooled in a reducing environment)

INTERIOR SURFACE COLOR: dark gray (10YR 4/1)

EXTERIOR SURFACE COLOR: black (10YR 2/1)

WALL THICKNESS: 5.9 mm at the neck and 6.3 mm on the body

INTERIOR SURFACE TREATMENT: burnished on upper neck

EXTERIOR SURFACE TREATMENT: burnished

HEIGHT: 22.2 cm   ORIFICE DIAMETER: 5.3 cm at the neck

DIAMETER AT BOTTOM OF RIM OR NECK: 10.5 cm on the body

BASE DIAMETER: 6.7 cm

ESTIMATED VOLUME: 0.6 liters

DECORATION: The vessel body has a diagonally-oriented engraved canebrake rattlesnake motif (Figure 54) repeated twice as they curve around the vessel in a diagonal S-shape (Hart 1982:59), and a red clay pigment has been rubbed in the engraved lines. The rattlesnake motif includes a circular head with a forked tongue (Figure 55), dots for eyes, two other dots for the nose, cross-hatched diamond-shaped areas on the body, and a bulbous hatched tail or rattle. The engraved rattlesnakes are separated from one another by four diagonal scrolls with hatched and cross-hatched zones and circles. Within each circle in these scroll elements is a smaller second circle with intersecting engraved lines with small hatched pendant triangles.

TYPE: Nacogdoches Engraved (Hart 1982: Figure 3-8a). The engraved rattlesnake motif is known on pottery vessels from at least 16 sites in eastern Texas and southwestern Arkansas (Walters 2006: Figure 16), but examples are primarily concentrated into Big Cypress and Sabine clusters, suggesting the vessel from the Washington Square Mound site may have been obtained in trade from Caddo groups living in those two areas to the north.

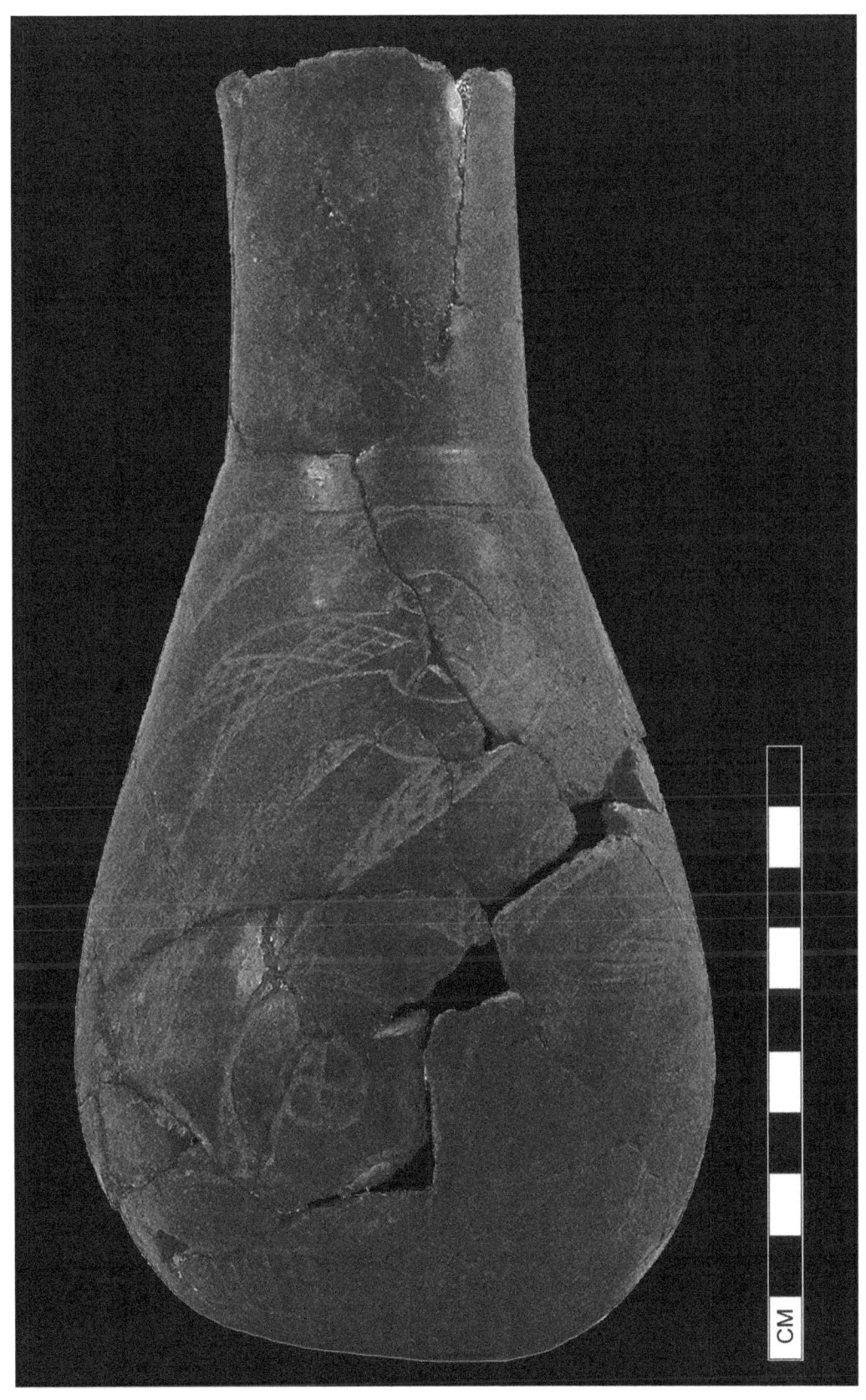

Figure 54. Nacogdoches Engraved bottle, F95-23.

SITE NO.: 41NA49

FEATURE: 95

VESSEL NO.: F95-25

NON-PLASTICS: grog and charred organic remains

VESSEL FORM: Bowl with a direct rim and a rounded, exterior folded lip

CORE COLOR: F (fired in a reducing environment and cooled in the open air)

INTERIOR SURFACE COLOR: dark reddish-gray (5YR 4/2) on the rim and yellowish-red (5YR 5/6) on the body

EXTERIOR SURFACE COLOR: yellowish-red (5YR 5/6)

WALL THICKNESS: 4.6 mm

INTERIOR SURFACE TREATMENT: smoothed on the rim and body

EXTERIOR SURFACE TREATMENT: burnished

HEIGHT: 8.5 cm

ORIFICE DIAMETER: 14.0 cm

DIAMETER AT BOTTOM OF RIM OR NECK: 12.3 cm

BASE DIAMETER: 7.5 cm

ESTIMATED VOLUME: 0.5 liters

DECORATION: Scroll and circle motif repeated four times around the vessel rim (Figure 55). Each of the central circles has a single very small circle or dot within it; the central circles are connected by curved diagonal engraved lines. The upper and lower triangular-shaped scroll elements (five pairs) are hatched.

TYPE: Nacogdoches Engraved (Hart 1982: Figure 3-5d).

Figure 55. Nacogdoches Engraved bowl, F95-25.

Documentation of Associated and Unassociated Caddo Funerary Objects

SITE NO.: 41NA49

FEATURE: F95

VESSEL NO.: F95-26

NON-PLASTICS: bone

VESSEL FORM: Carinated bowl with a direct rim and a rounded, exterior folded, lip (Figure 56)

CORE COLOR: F (fired in a reducing environment and cooled in the open air)

INTERIOR SURFACE COLOR: light yellowish-brown (10YR 6/4)

EXTERIOR SURFACE COLOR: yellowish-brown (10YR 5/4) with dark brown (10YR 3/3) fire clouds

WALL THICKNESS: 5.7 mm; the base is 8.4 mm thick

INTERIOR SURFACE TREATMENT: smoothed

EXTERIOR SURFACE TREATMENT: smoothed

HEIGHT: 11.5 cm

ORIFICE DIAMETER: 17.0 cm

DIAMETER AT BOTTOM OF RIM OR NECK: 19.5 cm

BASE DIAMETER: 9.5 cm

ESTIMATED VOLUME: 1.2 liters

DECORATION: Plain

TYPE: Undetermined (Hart 1982:86). Hart (1982:86) incorrectly labeled this vessel as F95-24, which in actuality appears to be part of vessel F95-19 (see above).

Figure 56. Plain carinated bowl, F95-26.

Documentation of Associated and Unassociated Caddo Funerary Objects

SITE NO.: 41NA49

FEATURE: 95

VESSEL NO.: F95-27

NON-PLASTICS: grog

VESSEL FORM: Bottle with a straight neck, direct rim, and rounded lip; there are four evenly-spaced peaks on the body midway between the bottom of the neck and the bottle base (Figure 57).

CORE COLOR: F (fired in a reducing environment and cooled in the open air)

INTERIOR SURFACE COLOR: brown (10YR 4/3) to dark brown (10YR 3/3)

EXTERIOR SURFACE COLOR: dark brown (10YR 3/3) to black (10YR 2/1)

WALL THICKNESS: 5.0 mm on the neck and 4.0 mm on the body

INTERIOR SURFACE TREATMENT: smoothed on the neck

EXTERIOR SURFACE TREATMENT: burnished

HEIGHT: 15.5 cm

ORIFICE DIAMETER: 4.7 cm

DIAMETER AT BOTTOM OF RIM OR NECK: 4.9 cm

BASE DIAMETER: 7.5 cm

ESTIMATED VOLUME: 0.5 liters

DECORATION: The body has engraved concentric circles repeated four times around the vessel; the concentric circles are centered on the body peaks. Each concentric circle has alternating cross-hatched zones and fine lines, and the outer cross-hatched zone has either six to eight excised spurs, suggesting "a sun-like appearance" (Hart 1982:60). The concentric circle motifs are divided by hour glass-shaped engraved elements with narrow nested cross-hatched outlined circles, cross-hatched triangles, and horizontal cross-hatched zones (Figure 57).

TYPE: Nacogdoches Engraved (Hart 1982: Figure 3-8b).

Figure 57. Nacogdoches Engraved bottle, F95-27.

Documentation of Associated and Unassociated Caddo Funerary Objects

SITE NO.: 41NA49

FEATURE: 95

VESSEL NO.: F95-28

NON-PLASTICS: grog with a sandy paste

VESSEL FORM: Jar with a direct rim and a rounded lip

CORE COLOR: G (fired in a reducing environment and cooled in the open air)

INTERIOR SURFACE COLOR: dark reddish-gray (5YR 4/2)

EXTERIOR SURFACE COLOR: yellowish-red (5YR 5/6)

WALL THICKNESS: 8.8 mm on the rim and 8.2 mm on the body

INTERIOR SURFACE TREATMENT: smoothed; charred organic residue on the upper body

EXTERIOR SURFACE TREATMENT: none

HEIGHT: 14.6 cm

ORIFICE DIAMETER: 12.8 cm

DIAMETER AT BOTTOM OF RIM OR NECK: N/A

BASE DIAMETER: 8.8 cm

ESTIMATED VOLUME: 1.1 liters

DECORATION: The rim has an incised-punctated scroll and circle motif repeated twice around the vessel. The upper and lower parts of the scroll and the central circle are filled with tool punctations (Figure 58).

TYPE: Undetermined incised-punctated vessel, possible local variety of Crockett Curvilinear Incised (Hart 1982:90 and Figure 3-15c).

Figure 58. Undetermined incised-punctated jar, F95-28.

Documentation of Associated and Unassociated Caddo Funerary Objects

SITE NO.: 41NA49

FEATURE: 95

VESSEL NO.: F95-29

NON-PLASTICS: grog and hematite

VESSEL FORM: Carinated bowl with a direct rim and a rounded, slightly exterior folded, lip

CORE COLOR: F (fired in a reducing environment and cooled in the open air)

INTERIOR SURFACE COLOR: reddish-brown (2.5YR 4/4)

EXTERIOR SURFACE COLOR: reddish-brown (2.5YR 4/4)

WALL THICKNESS: rim is 5.7 mm thick and the body is 6.4 mm thick

INTERIOR SURFACE TREATMENT: smoothed on the rim

EXTERIOR SURFACE TREATMENT: smoothed

HEIGHT: 7.5 cm

ORIFICE DIAMETER: 14.8 cm

DIAMETER AT BOTTOM OF RIM OR NECK: 13.6 cm

BASE DIAMETER: 6.0 cm

ESTIMATED VOLUME: 0.7 liters

DECORATION: There are upper and lower horizontal incised lines on the rim, one under the lip and the other at the carination. The rim itself has four panels each filled with a single and centrally-placed horizontal row of tool punctations (Figure 59). The panels are divided by hour glass-shaped elements filled with diagonal hatched incised lines.

TYPE: Washington Square Paneled (Hart 1982:73-74 and Figure 3-12c).

Figure 59. Washington Square Paneled carinated bowl, F95-29.

Documentation of Associated and Unassociated Caddo Funerary Objects

SITE NO.: 41NA49

FEATURE: 95

VESSEL NO.: F95-30

NON-PLASTICS: hematite, grog, and bone

VESSEL FORM: Carinated bowl with a direct rim and a rounded lip (Figure 60)

CORE COLOR: G (fired in a reducing environment and cooled in the open air)

INTERIOR SURFACE COLOR: very dark brown (10YR 2/2) to black (10YR 2/1); organic residue

EXTERIOR SURFACE COLOR: brown (7.5YR 4/4); organic residue

WALL THICKNESS: 7.7 mm; the base is 13.3 mm thick

INTERIOR SURFACE TREATMENT: smoothed

EXTERIOR SURFACE TREATMENT: smoothed

HEIGHT: 11.0 cm

ORIFICE DIAMETER: 29.5 cm

DIAMETER AT BOTTOM OF RIM OR NECK: 26.0 cm

BASE DIAMETER: 9.0 cm

ESTIMATED VOLUME: 1.95 liters

DECORATION: Plain

TYPE: Undetermined plain ware vessel (Hart 1982:85).

Figure 60. Plain carinated bowl, F95-30.

Documentation of Associated and Unassociated Caddo Funerary Objects

SITE NO.: 41NA49

FEATURE: 95

VESSEL NO.: F95-31

NON-PLASTICS: bone and grog

VESSEL FORM: Carinated bowl with an everted rim and a rounded lip (Figure 61)

CORE COLOR: Undetermined, but probably A (fired and cooled in an oxidizing environment)

INTERIOR SURFACE COLOR: reddish-yellow (7.5YR 6/6)

EXTERIOR SURFACE COLOR: yellowish-red (5YR 5/8)

WALL THICKNESS: 5.7 mm

INTERIOR SURFACE TREATMENT: burnished

EXTERIOR SURFACE TREATMENT: burnished

HEIGHT: 7.0 cm

ORIFICE DIAMETER: 15.5 cm

DIAMETER AT BOTTOM OF RIM OR NECK: 12.5 cm

BASE DIAMETER: 6.0 cm

ESTIMATED VOLUME: 0.7 liters

DECORATION: Plain

TYPE: Undetermined plain ware vessel (Hart 1982:86).

Figure 61. Plain carinated bowl, F95-31.

Documentation of Associated and Unassociated Caddo Funerary Objects

SITE NO.: 41NA49

FEATURE: 95

VESSEL NO.: F95-32

NON-PLASTICS: grog, bone, and hematite

VESSEL FORM: Carinated bowl with a direct rim with a Redwine mode pie-crust lip (Figure 62a-b)

CORE COLOR: F (fired in a reducing environment and cooled in the open air)

INTERIOR SURFACE COLOR: yellowish-red (5YR 4/6); fire cloud on base

EXTERIOR SURFACE COLOR: very dark gray (5YR 3/1), except on the lip, where it is yellowish-red (5YR 4/6)

WALL THICKNESS: 6.2 mm

INTERIOR SURFACE TREATMENT: smoothed on body and rim

EXTERIOR SURFACE TREATMENT: smoothed to burnished on the body and rim

HEIGHT: 7.5 cm

ORIFICE DIAMETER: 23.5 cm

DIAMETER AT BOTTOM OF RIM OR NECK: 18.1 cm

BASE DIAMETER: 8.0 cm

ESTIMATED VOLUME: 1.1 liters

DECORATION: An engraved scroll and circle motif is repeated eight times around the vessel rim (Figure 62a). There are hatched pendant triangles or fill zones above and below each of the multi-lined scrolls, and the central circle is formed by repeated circular lines, and there is a small hatched circle in the center of the main circular element.

TYPE: Nacogdoches Engraved (Hart 1982: Figure 3-6d).

Figure 62a. Nacogdoches Engraved carinated bowl, F95-32, side view.

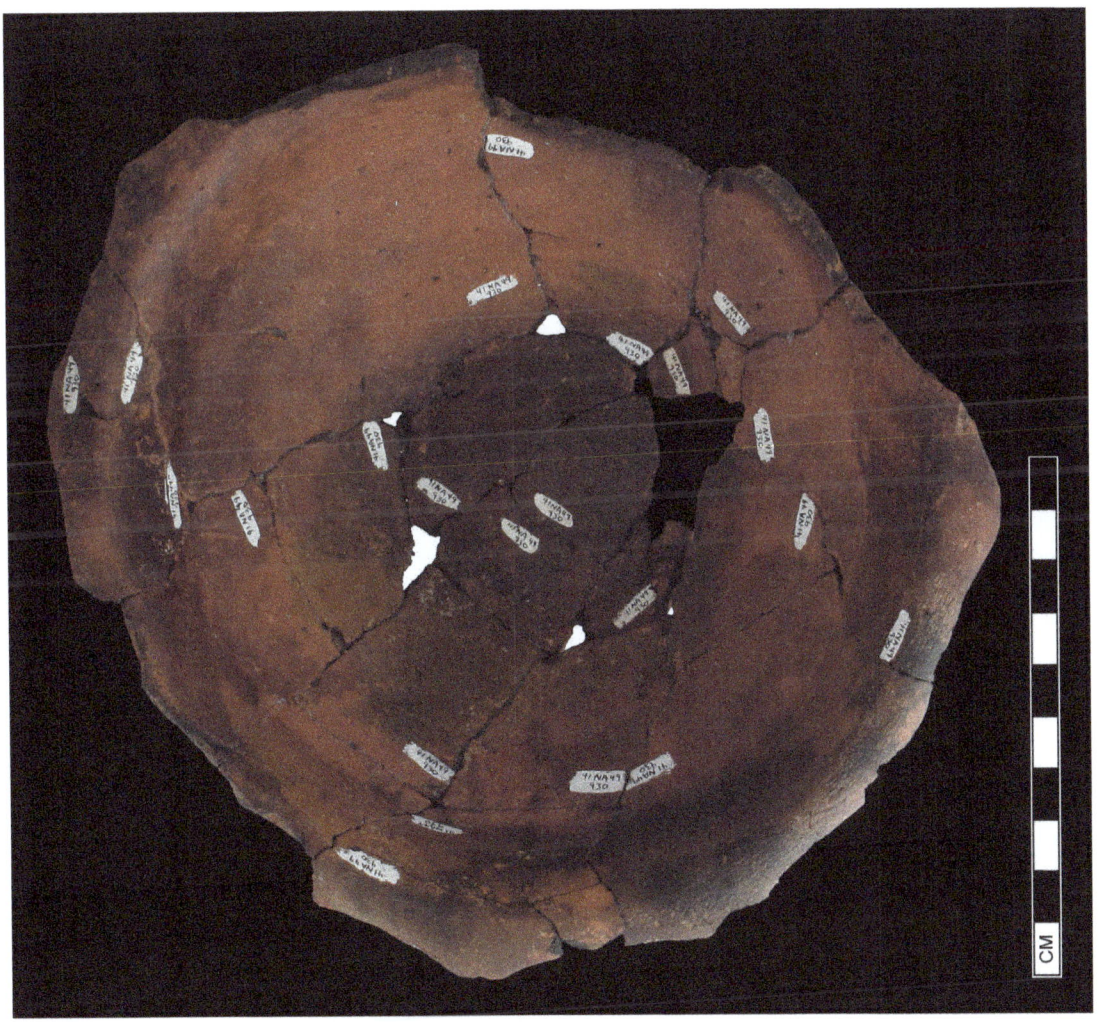

Figure 62b. Nacogdoches Engraved carinated bowl, F95-32, view of Redwine mode rim.

Documentation of Associated and Unassociated Caddo Funerary Objects

SITE NO.: 41NA49

FEATURE: 95

VESSEL NO.: F95-33

NON-PLASTICS: grog and bone

VESSEL FORM: Carinated bowl with a direct rim and a rounded lip

CORE COLOR: F (fired in a reducing environment and cooled in the open air)

INTERIOR SURFACE COLOR: strong brown (7.5YR 5/6)

EXTERIOR SURFACE COLOR: brown (7.5YR 5/4)

WALL THICKNESS: 6.4 mm; the base is 13.3 mm thick

INTERIOR SURFACE TREATMENT: burnished

EXTERIOR SURFACE TREATMENT: burnished

HEIGHT: 13.5 cm

ORIFICE DIAMETER: 27.0 cm

DIAMETER AT BOTTOM OF RIM OR NECK: 27.0 cm

BASE DIAMETER: 9.0 cm

ESTIMATED VOLUME: 3.2 liters

DECORATION: A tool punctated scroll and circle motif (the *Crockett* scroll) is repeated six times around the vessel rim (Figure 63). There are punctated and punctate-filled pendant fill zones or areas above and below each of the scrolls, and the central circle is formed by a single punctated circular line, and this circle is also filled with punctations.

TYPE: Hart (1982:54-55 and Figure 3-6c) identifies this vessel as Nacogdoches Engraved. Because the motif is executed strictly with punctations, this vessel should either be differentiated as a distinct variety of Nacogdoches Engraved that is kept separate from vessels decorated with engraved lines, or this particular punctated scroll vessel may be separated as a distinct and new type, perhaps Nacogdoches Punctated.

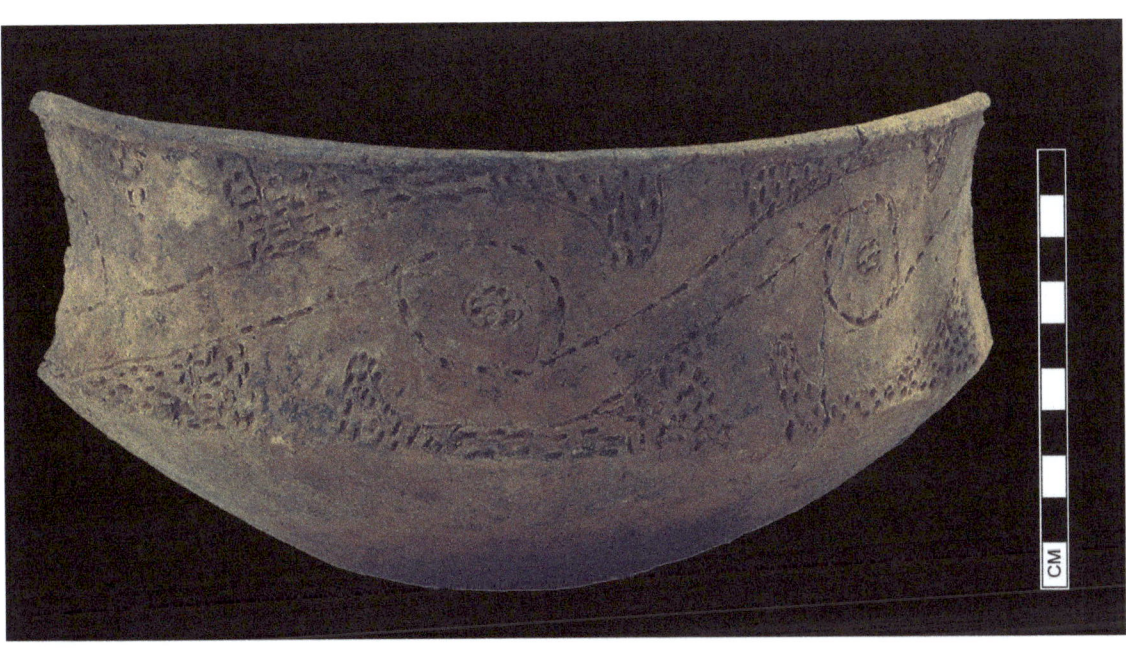

Figure 63. Nacogdoches Engraved, nee Nacogdoches Punctated carinated bowl, F95-33.

Documentation of Associated and Unassociated Caddo Funerary Objects

SITE NO.: 41NA49

FEATURE: 95

VESSEL NO.: F95-34

NON-PLASTICS: bone and grog

VESSEL FORM: Globular or compound bowl with an everted rim and a rounded lip

CORE COLOR: G (fired in a reducing environment and cooled in the open air)

INTERIOR SURFACE COLOR: dark brown (7.5YR 3/2)

EXTERIOR SURFACE COLOR: strong brown (7.5YR 4/6)

WALL THICKNESS: rim is 5.7 mm thick, the body is 6.5 mm thick, and the base is 5.6 mm in thickness

INTERIOR SURFACE TREATMENT: burnished

EXTERIOR SURFACE TREATMENT: burnished

HEIGHT: 11.6 cm

ORIFICE DIAMETER: 17.0 cm

DIAMETER AT BOTTOM OF RIM OR NECK: N/A

BASE DIAMETER: 5.1 cm

ESTIMATED VOLUME: 1.1 liters

DECORATION: The upper rim panel has a single horizontal engraved line on it (Figure 64). The lower panel has engraved semi-circles or concentric filled with a circular element that are repeated three times on the vessel. These are surrounded by fill elements comprised of negative circles and negative S-shaped areas demarcated by horizontal or diagonal hatched lines. The central circular engraved element has hatched pendant triangles and a central engraved dot, and there are three smaller versions of the circular engraved element within the fill areas in the upper part of the lower panel.

TYPE: Nacogdoches Engraved (Hart 1982: Figure 3-8c).

Figure 64. Nacogdoches Engraved compound bowl, F95-34.

Appendix 2

Preliminary Report on the Skeletal Analysis of Burials from the Washington Square Mound Site (41NA49) in Nacogdoches County, Texas*

Preliminary Report on the Skeletal Analysis of Burials from the Washington Square Mound Site (41NA49) in Nacogdoches County, Texas*

Robert G. Franciscus

Texas A&M University, March 1985

Abstract

This paper provides a preliminary report on the skeletal analysis of burials from the Washington Square Mound site (41NA49) in Nacogdoches County, Texas. The Caddo mound site, excavated under the supervision of Dr. James E. Corbin of Stephen F. Austin University during three field seasons from 1979 to 1981, contained three burials, two of which when excavated, yielded a total of three individuals. Analysis of the remains indicates a young adult female, tall in stature, exhibiting intentional cultural cranial deformation and porotic hyperostosis; a young adult male, short in stature, also exhibiting marked intentional cultural cranial deformation; and a young male probably in his late teens. The remains of these three individuals collectively exhibit many of the features generally found in skeletal material from Caddo burials such as multiple burials, cultural cranial deformation, low levels of dental attrition and a tendency towards increased dental caries and ante-mortem tooth loss.

Introduction

The Washington Square Mound site is located in Nacogdoches County in East Texas, thirty miles east of the George C. Davis site. This Caddo mound site is located in an early residential area known as Washington Square, which is located in the center of Nacogdoches, Texas, the county seat (Corbin 1980).

Investigations of the site began in the spring of 1979 under Dr. James E. Corbin of Stephen F. Austin University. Late in the season the investigators decided to excavate a test trench into the Reavely-House Mound, located across from the Thomas J. Rusk Middle School. The purpose of this trench was to determine the original size and construction of the mound. Previously, one shallow burial, Feature 31, was excavated that year and two other burial pits were discovered in the process of excavating the trench. In the 1980 season, a trench was excavated on the east side of the mound revealing two more burial pits, Feature 95 and Feature 90. However, due to time constraints, neither Feature 95 or 90 was excavated. During the 1981 season Feature 95 was excavated to learn more about the mortuary practices at the site and to enlarge their ceramic vessel collection to help the investigators assess the cultural-historical relationships of this site in the Caddo tradition (McDonald 1981).

The sample for this analysis, which was recovered from two excavated burials, consists of three individuals. Feature 95 contained two individuals, buried in an extended supine position with their heads facing southeast. Additionally, one individual was placed on top of the other. Feature 31 contained a third individual also buried in an extended supine position with the head facing southeast. Both burials contained a large wealth of ceramics and other artifacts. At the time of excavation, the burial matrix, skeletal material and ceramics were very moist. All indications were that since a recent razing of the ground, the lower portion of the pit was often extremely wet.

Materials and Methods

Bone preservation was uniformly poor. The remains of Feature 95 consisted of both cranial and post-cranial material. Remains of both individuals are numerous, but fragmentary. The remains of Feature 31 were scanty, consisting of cranial fragments and 15 isolated teeth.

Visual inspection of the remains was utilized to determine sex and age as well as any discernable pathology. Due to the fragmentary nature of the remains, quantitative analysis, such as anthropometric measurements were not possible. Stature estimations for the two individuals contained in Feature 95 were determined by comparison with complete long bones from study samples at Texas A&M University which exhibited similar size and morphology to the incomplete bones (in this case the femur for Individual 1 and the radius for Individual 2). The most comparable complete bones were then measured, and this measurement used to estimate stature based on Genoves' (1967) formulae for estimating stature among Mesoamericans. It is important to note that this technique utilizes comparisons between skeletal components from two distinct populations and thus the stature estimations which are derived are at best only approximations.

Sex determination criteria for this sample utilized cranial and post-cranial indicators when possible (Feature 95, Individual 1) and cranial indicators alone (Feature 95, Individual 1; Feature 31, Individual 3). These included: the angle of the greater sciatic notch; the morphology and degree of robusticity of the mandible (specifically the appearance of the mental symphasis and the ascending ramus); the gonial angle when possible; and the extension, as a crest, of the posterior portion of the zygomatic process of the temporal.

Age was based primarily on dental evidence, utilizing such indicators as the eruption of key teeth (such as the third molar and the pre-molars) as well as the subsequent wear on all the dentition. Four categories of dental wear were utilized (Commuzie 1982): light, characterized by a polishing and smoothing of the occlusal surface; moderate, characterized by some loss of the enamel from the occlusal surface, exposing the dentine; heavy, characterized by loss of all the enamel from the occlusal surface; and very heavy, which is characterized by total loss of the enamel from the occlusal surface in conjunction with reshaping of the tooth. In fact, only two of these categories (light and moderate) were exhibited by the present sample.

Other indicators of age were utilized when possible such as epiphyseal fusion, or non-fusion of key bones such as the sternal portion of the clavicle (Feature 95, Individual 1).

Results

This material constitutes what appears to be a rather homogenous sample, with very little sexual dimorphism. The sample, however, is small and undoubtedly biased. Two individuals exhibit marked intentional cultural cranial deformation of the fronto-occipital type. Also found in this sample were dental pathologies and anomalies, and skeletal pathology. Each individual is detailed in the text with respect to sex, age, dentition, and other specifics.

Since age determination in this sample is derived, in great part, using dental analysis, it should be noted that dental attrition in itself is only a relative indicator of age. Dental attrition varies from population to population, in part, due to differing diets and subsistence technologies. The use of wooden mortars and pestles, for instance, rather than stone grinders for pounding dried maize into meal resulted in lighter wear on Caddo dentition (Powell and Rogers 1980). This should be noted in light of the fact that dental attrition was light on all three individuals in this sample.

Feature 95, Individual 1

The remains of Individual 1 consists of both cranial and post-cranial material (Table A-1). Remains are numerous but fragmentary and in poor condition.

This individual appears to be a young adult female. Sex was determined by cranial and post-cranial indicators. Portions of both the left and right innominate contained a major portion of the sciatic notch exhibiting the wide, less acute angle, usually indicative of females. Although somewhat squared, the overall appearance of the mandible is gracile. The mental symphysis is more rounded and less squared than in the other individual in this burial (Individual 2). Additionally, the ascending ramus is comparatively less rugose. The posterior portion of the zygomatic process does not extend, as a crest, as far back in this individual, ending generally above the external auditory meatus for both left and right sides. Finally, a relatively complete right femur, although exhibiting considerable post-mortem damage and indicative of a relatively tall person, nonetheless appears to be very gracile.

Table A-1. Bone Inventory.

Individual 1 (Feature 95)

B48	left parietal fragment
	right parietal fragment
	frontal fragment
	occipital fragment
	left parietal fragment
	right parietal fragment
B54	basilar occipital fragment
	inferior septum fragment
B41	right temporal fragment
B42	left temporal fragment
B43	right maxilla
	left maxilla
B40	mandible
B44	atlas (cervical 1)
	axis (cervical 2)
	cervical vertebra fragment
	cervical vertebra fragment
	thoracic vertebra fragment
	thoracic vertebra fragment
	thoracic vertebra fragment
	thoracic vertebra fragment
	thoracic vertebra fragment
	thoracic vertebra fragment
	thoracic vertebra fragment
	thoracic vertebra fragment
	lumbar vertebra fragment
B46	right clavicle
	left sternal clavicle
B47	left rib (1)
	right rib (1)
	rib fragments
B18	right scapula fragment
	right scapula fragment
B21	left humerus shaft fragment
	left humerus distal shaft fragment
B39	right scaphoid
B17	right innominate fragment
B19	right innominate fragment
B23	left innominate fragment
B25	right femur

Table A-1. Bone Inventory, cont.

Individual 1 (Feature 95) (cont.)

B24	left proximal femur
B27	left distal femur
B26	right proximal tibia
B37	right talus
	right calcaneous
	right navicular
	right metatarsal fragment
	right metatarsal fragment
B38	left talus
	left metatarsal fragment
	left metatarsal fragment

Individual 2 (Feature 95)

B28	frontal
B30	right temporal fragment
B37	right zygomatic malar fragment
B33	left temporal fragment
	right maxilla
B32	left maxilla
B31	basilar occipital
B36	occipital
B29	mandible
B34	axis (cervical 2)
	cervical vertebra fragment
	cervical vertebra fragment
	cervical vertebra fragment
	cervical vertebra fragment
	cervical vertebra fragment
	cervical vertebra fragment
	cervical vertebra fragment
B39	right rib (1)
B11	left rib (1)
B7	rib fragment
B40	manubrium
B10	right scapula fragment
B38	left scapula fragment
B5	right distal ulna
B14	left distal ulna

Table A-1. Bone Inventory, cont.

Individual 2 (Feature 95) (cont.)

B2	right scaphoid
	right trapezoid
	right metacarpal fragment
B12	left metacarpal (2)
	left metacarpal (5)
B1	right innominate fragment
B15	right innominate fragment
B6	sacrum fragment
B16	right proximal femur
B42	metatarsal fragment

Individual 3 (Feature 31)

B54-1	right parietal
	frontal fragment
B54-2	left temporal fragment
B54-3	right temporal fragment (petrous)
B54-4	left temporal fragment (petrous)
B54-5	cranial fragments

At the time of death Individual 1 was probably between 20-30 years of age. Fully erupted and lightly worn third molars in the mandible and maxilla indicate adulthood. Eleven of 17 teeth in this individual for which wear can be determined exhibit light wear. The remaining teeth exhibit moderate wear (Table A-2). The absence of heavy wear in the dentition of this individual and the relatively high percentage of teeth exhibiting light wear tends to support the designation of this individual as a young adult. Finally, the sternal portion of both the left and right scapulae exhibit an unfused epiphysis. Fusion of this bone normally occurs between the age of 25 and 30 (McKern and Stewart 1957).

The dentition of Individual 1 exhibits shoveling on both medial upper incisors, a common feature of North American Indian groups (Dahlberg 1951). Numerous dental pathologies occur in this individual. LM_3 and RM_3 are extremely maloccluded with both teeth inclined lingually (RM_3 approximately 90% and LM_3 approximately 45%). The result of this malocclusion was that the buccal aspect of both molars became the occlusal surface, with the greatest wear occurring there. RM^1 exhibits a severe caries. Except for a small portion of the mesio-buccal and disto-lingual surface, the entire crown has been destroyed. An associated abscess can be seen in the alveolar process, evidenced by a large, clearly defined circular hole, with concise rounded margins. More moderate caries occur on the LM_3, RM_3, and the RM^3. Ante-mortem evulsion of at least two and possibly four mandibular molars occurred in this individual. LM_1 and RM_2 were evulsed in that order as evidenced by the subsequent degree of refilling of the alveolus. RM_1 and LM_2, although not found with the remains, could conceivably have been lost post-mortem, however, evidence for the beginning and intermediate phases of refilling of the alveolus for both teeth indicate that ante-mortem loss is as likely. The resorption and remodeling of the mandible in this individual is due to the ante-mortem loss of molars just described. This gives the appearance of an aged mandible, which in light of all the preceding evidence is definitely not the case.

Table A-2. Dentition.

Tooth	F95 Individual 1	F95 Individual 2	F31, Individual 3
LI^1	M, SH, I	M	-
RI^1	M, SH, I	M	-
LI^2	-	L	-
RI^2	-	L	-
LC^1	M, I	L	-
RC^1	M, I	L	L, I
LPM^1	L	L	L, I
RPM^1	L	L	L, I
LPM^2	L	L	*, I
RPM^2	M	L	L, I
LM^1	L	M, C	L, I
RM^1	SC	M, C	L, I
LM^2	L	L	L, I
RM^2	L	L	L, I
LM^3	-	L	unerupted, I
RM^3	L, C	L	unerupted, I
LI_1	-	M	-
RI_1	-	M	-
LI_2	-	M	-
RI_2	-	M	-
LC_1	-	M	-
RC_1	-	M	-
LPM_1	-	L	L, I
RPM_1	M	L	-
LPM_2	L	L	-
RPM_2	L	L	-
LM_1	-	L, C	L, I, P
RM_1	-	L	-
LM_2	-	L	L, I, P
RM_2	-	L	-
LM_3	L, C	L, C	L, I, P
RM_3	L, C	L	-

*=undetermined wear; L=light wear; M=moderate wear; SH=shovel-shaped; C=caries, SC=severe caries; I=isolated; P=protostylid

Porotic hyperostosis is also evident in this individual. Although there is considerable post-mortem damage to the cranial remains (consisting of large portions of the left and right parietal and small portions of the frontal and occipital), widening of the diploe, thinning of the outer table, and the presence of small apertures on the cranial surface both internally and externally indicate this pathology.

Intentional cranial deformation of the cranium is evident for Individual 1. The posterior portion of the cranium in the area of the superior portion of the lambdoidal suture is flattened markedly.

The stature estimation (167 cm) obtained for this individual indicates a female significantly taller than the mean height projected by Genoves' formulae (Table A-3).

Table A-3. Stature estimates for Individuals 1 and 2 (Feature 95) utilizing complete bones from study samples. All measurements in mm.

Individual 1 (Female)	Individual 2 (Male)
R. femur: fairly complete proximal portion and entire shaft, however, missing distal portion including both condyles and epicondyles, as well as several landmarks on portion that is present	L. Radius: distal portion only including styloid process and staphoid surface and portion of shaft
Compared to:	Compared to:
R. femur: from male (78-1 Hinton Ruin, Burial 68) complete, measured 46.2	L. Radius: from male (78-1 Hinton Ruin Burial 12) complete, measured 25.2
Genoves' stature estimation for Femur: 46.2=167.00	L. Radius: sex not known (Texas A&M University teaching collection) complete, measured 21.6
*male and female femora were compared in this case because no female femora comparable in length to Individual 1 were available	mean of both=23.4 Genoves' stature estimation for radius: 23.4=160.50 *two radii were used because there was not a good correlation for each individually. This estimate is probably not as accurate as that for Individual 1

Documentation of Associated and Unassociated Caddo Funerary Objects

Feature 95, Individual 2

The remains of Individual 2 consist of both cranial and post-cranial material (see Table A-1). As with Individual 1, remains are numerous but fragmentary.

This individual appears to be a young adult male based upon features of the cranium. The appearance of the mandible is robust and squared, with a gonial angle of 119 degrees (this measurement is approximated slightly due to a small amount of post-mortem damage to the gonial angle). The posterior portion of the zygomatic process extends further back in this individual, ending well beyond the external auditory meatus in both temporal fragments.

The age for this individual was determined exclusively by dentition. Fully erupted third molars in both the mandible and maxilla indicate adulthood. All 32 teeth were intact in this individual, with 22 of the 32 teeth (69%) exhibiting light wear (see Table A-2). This high percentage of light wear as well as the complete absence of heavy wear and virtually no wear on all four third molars indicate a young adult. As with Individual 1, shoveling is present on both upper medial incisors. Minor caries are evident on LM^1, RM^1, LM_1, and LM_3. There is a curious wear pattern in this individual isolated to four teeth: LM^1 and RM^1 exhibit greater wear on the lingual portion of the tooth, resulting in wear slanting towards the buccal aspect. The exact opposite pattern is present in the occluding mandibular teeth, LM_1 and RM_1, where the wear slants up towards the lingual aspect. The wear pattern itself is not exceptional; however, the fact that it is isolated to these two pairs of occluding teeth is peculiar. Besides the minor incidence of caries noted, there was no evidence of periodontal infection or other dental pathology.

There is no indication of skeletal pathology in Individual 2. There are, however, two peculiar recessed, darkened pits evident: one occurs on the interior superior portion of the right orbit, and the other is on the rim of the head of the right femur. Both are oval and approximately 1 cm long. It is possible that these are metastatic lesions, however, it is more likely that these are due to a plant root in the burial, or other soil deposition. In any case, the poor condition of the bone impedes positive assessment.

Intentional cultural deformation of the cranium is evident in Individual 2. The frontal is conspicuously angular and marked by a recessed area where the frontal eminences normally occur, and a bulge or eminence very close to the coronal suture. An intact portion of the left parietal attached to the frontal exhibits a wide lateral flare. These two anomalies are indicative of fronto-occipital deformation.

The stature estimation derived for this individual (160.50 cm) indicates a relatively short individual, shorter in fact than the female, Individual 1 (see Table A-3).

Feature 31, Individual 3

The remains of Individual 3 are scanty and fragmentary, consisting of portions of the cranium, several cranial fragments (see Table A-1) and 15 isolated teeth (see Table A-2).

This individual appears to be a young male probably in his late teens at the time of death. Determination of sex in this individual is based on admittedly scanty evidence, the sole indicator being a portion of the left temporal. In comparison to the other two individuals in this sample, the posterior portion of the zygomatic process extends further back in this individual than in Individual 1 (female) and is comparable to the morphology exhibited by Individual 2 (male).

The age of this individual, while derived exclusively from dentition, is based on better evidence than the foregoing determination of gender. LM^3 and RM^3 were examined under a microscope for evidence of wear facets. Both occlusal and interstitial aspects were examined and an extremely small wear facet is noticeable on the disto-buccal cusp. the wear is slight and cannot be seen with the unaided eye; this tooth, therefore, had probably just begun to erupt at the time of death. Wear facets on three of the four pre-molars examined are evident both on occlusal and interstitial surfaces (this evidence for wear, again found under the microscope, was important because all pre-molars for this individual were eroded enamel shells, missing both dentine and root structure and in fact, to the unaided eye appeared to be immature tooth buds). It is important to note that virtually all wear found on this individual's teeth was extremely slight. Based on the foregoing dental evidence, therefore, this individual was probably just approaching adulthood.

Two further aspects of this individual's dentition are worth noting. First, is the condition of some of the teeth alluded to above. Fourteen of 15 teeth examined were missing roots entirely and five of these were also missing dentine so that in effect all that remained of these teeth were enamel shells. This peculiar condition is probably a result of the poor preservation of this individual in general rather than a pathology. Second, LM_3, LM_2, and LM_1 all contain a protostylid: an extra cusp that occurs on the anterior aspect of the buccal surface of the mandibular molars. It is prominent and well defined on LM_3, less so on LM_2 and barely present on LM_1.

Conclusions

The remains of these three individuals from the Washington Square Mound site exhibit many of the features generally found in skeletal material from Caddo burials. Artificial cranial deformation, evident in two of the individuals in this sample, may not have been practiced universally by the Caddos, but the custom apparently was an old one, observed prehistorically in the Texas area. For example, multiple burials have been found at the Sanders site near the Red River in Lamar County in which skulls show that fronto-occipital deformation was in vogue (Krieger 1946).

The low level of dental attrition exhibited by all three individuals, which is due in great part to the relatively young age of all three, nonetheless exhibits the low level of wear generally associated with the Caddo diet; apparently, the use of wooden mortars and pestles, rather than stone grinders, resulted in less grit content of foodstuffs and therefore less dental attrition. On the other hand, the soft maize breads, gruel, and mush of the Caddo diet were more likely to remain trapped in dental fissures and to decay and promote bacterial activity. As a result the Caddo population, in general, suffered more severely from dental caries and ante-mortem tooth loss (Powell and Rogers 1980). This condition is exhibited in Individual 1 (Feature 95). Both severe caries, resulting in periodontal infection and ante-mortem evulsion of mandibular molars, occurred in this relatively young female.

The occurrence of porotic hyperostosis in this same individual is interesting in light of the study by El-Najjar et al. (1976), correlating an increased dependence on maize by prehistoric and historic Anasazi Indians of the southwestern U.S. and a higher incidence of porotic hyperostosis. The hypothesis was that an increased dependence on maize produced more iron deficiency anemia and thus resulted in this particular pathology. The small size of the present sample inhibits any correlation between these items; however, if future excavations at this site produce more burial remains, it would be an interesting avenue of study.

References Cited

Corbin, J. E.
1980   Excavations at Washington Square Mound Site 1979. Paper presented at Caddo Conference, Stephen F. Austin University, Nacogdoches, Texas

Comuzzie, A. G.
1982   The Reconstruction and Analysis of Cranial Remains from the Palm Harbor (41AS80) in Aransas County, Texas. MS on file, Texas A&M University.

Dahlberg, A. A.
1951   The Dentition of the American Indian. In *The Physical Anthropology of the American Indian*, pp. 138-176. Viking Find, Inc., New York.

El-Najjar, M. Y., D. J. Ryan, C. G. Turner II, and B. Lozoff
1976   The Etiology of Porotic Hyperostosis among the Prehistoric and Historic Anasazi Indians of Southwestern United States. *American Journal of Physical Anthropology* 44:477-488.

Genoves, S.
1967   Proportionality of Long Limb Bones and Their Relation to Stature among Mesoamericans. *American Journal of Physical Anthropology* 26:67-78.

References Cited (cont.)

Krieger, A. D.
1946 *Culture Complexes and Chronology in Northern Texas.* Publication No. 4640. The University of Texas at Austin.

McDonald, J.
1981 Archaeological Investigations at the Reavely-House Mound. MS on file, Stephen F. Austin University, Nacogdoches.

McKern, T. W. and T. D. Stewart
1957 *Skeletal Age Change in Young American males, Analyzed from the Standpoint of Identification.* Technical Report EP-45. Headquarters Quartermaster Research and Development Command, Natick, Massachusetts.

Powell, M. L. and D. J. Rogers
1980 *Bioarcheology of the McCutchan-McLaughlin Site.* Studies in Oklahoma's Past No. 5. Oklahoma Archaeological Survey, Norman.

---

*For the current report, Franciscus' MS was lightly edited with respect to grammar and wording (i.e., "Caddoan" was changed uniformly to "Caddo").

Appendix 3

Vessel Recordation Forms for NAGPRA Collections from an Unknown East Texas Site or Sites and a Site at Greasy Creek in Camp County, Texas

Documentation of Associated and Unassociated Caddo Funerary Objects

SITE NO.: Unknown

FEATURE: None

VESSEL NO.: 31.1

NON-PLASTICS: bone

VESSEL FORM: bottle with a straight neck, an everted rim (emphasized by a horizontal line where the rim joins the neck), and a flat lip (Figure 65)

CORE COLOR: Undetermined

INTERIOR SURFACE COLOR: Undetermined

EXTERIOR SURFACE COLOR: light brownish-gray (10YR 6/2)

WALL THICKNESS: 5.8 mm

INTERIOR SURFACE TREATMENT: none

EXTERIOR SURFACE TREATMENT: smoothed

HEIGHT: 11.5 cm

ORIFICE DIAMETER: 4.2 cm

DIAMETER AT BOTTOM OF RIM OR NECK: 4.3 cm

BASE DIAMETER: 7.0 cm

ESTIMATED VOLUME: 0.3 liters

DECORATION: Plain

TYPE: Undetermined Caddo plain ware bottle

Figure 65. Vessel 31.1, a plain bottle, from an undetermined Caddo burial site.

Documentation of Associated and Unassociated Caddo Funerary Objects

SITE NO.: Unknown

FEATURE: None

VESSEL NO.: 31.2

NON-PLASTICS: none apparent

VESSEL FORM: Compound bowl with an everted rim and a rounded lip

CORE COLOR: B (fired and cooled in a reducing or low oxygen environment)

INTERIOR SURFACE COLOR: black (10YR 2/1)

EXTERIOR SURFACE COLOR: black (10YR 2/1)

WALL THICKNESS: 6.2 mm

INTERIOR SURFACE TREATMENT: smoothed

EXTERIOR SURFACE TREATMENT: burnished

HEIGHT: 9.2 cm

ORIFICE DIAMETER: 9.7 cm

DIAMETER AT BOTTOM OF RIM OR NECK: 7.8 cm

BASE DIAMETER: 6.0 cm

ESTIMATED VOLUME: 0.7 liters

DECORATION: The upper panel of the vessel has three broadly-spaced engraved lines. The lower panel has sets of concentric circles divided by vertical engraved arcs or parentheses (Figure 66). A red hematite-rich clay pigment has been rubbed in the engraved design.

TYPE: possible Wilder Engraved, a Late Caddo (ca. A.D. 1430-1680) Titus phase ceramic type (Suhm and Jelks 1962; Thurmond 1990).

Figure 66. Engraved compound bowl from unknown site, Vessel 31.2.

Documentation of Associated and Unassociated Caddo Funerary Objects

SITE NO.: Unknown

FEATURE: None

VESSEL NO.: 31.3

NON-PLASTICS: none apparent

VESSEL FORM: Carinated bowl with an inverted rim, and a rounded but exterior folded lip

CORE COLOR: Undetermined

INTERIOR SURFACE COLOR: light yellowish-brown (10YR 6/4)

EXTERIOR SURFACE COLOR: light yellowish-brown (10YR 6/4)

WALL THICKNESS: 8.1 cm

INTERIOR SURFACE TREATMENT: burnished

EXTERIOR SURFACE TREATMENT: burnished

HEIGHT: 14.0 cm

ORIFICE DIAMETER: 25.0 cm

DIAMETER AT BOTTOM OF RIM OR NECK: 26.5 cm

BASE DIAMETER: 8.0 cm

ESTIMATED VOLUME: 3.1 liters

DECORATION: Narrow engraved panels with three sets (six lines in each set) of short vertical engraved lines separated by undecorated areas. Each set of engraved lines is repeated twice on the vessel rim (Figure 67).

TYPE: Undetermined, but possibly Washington Square Paneled. According to the records on file at SFA, this vessel was donated (exactly when is not known) to SFA by J. F. Tidwell, a student there in the late 1920s. The vessel was apparently found near Alto, in Cherokee County, Texas.

Figure 67. Undetermined engraved carinated bowl from an unknown site in Cherokee County, Texas, Vessel 31.3.

SITE NO.: Unknown, but from Greasy Creek Area
(41CP71, see Perttula and Nelson 2004)

FEATURE: None   VESSEL NO.: 31.5

NON-PLASTICS: none apparent

VESSEL FORM: bowl with an everted rim and a rounded, but exterior folded lip

CORE COLOR: B (fired and cooled in a reducing environment)

INTERIOR SURFACE COLOR: brown (10YR 4/3)

EXTERIOR SURFACE COLOR: dark brown (10YR 3/3)

WALL THICKNESS: 5.8 mm

INTERIOR SURFACE TREATMENT: smoothed

EXTERIOR SURFACE TREATMENT: burnished

HEIGHT: 4.8 cm

ORIFICE DIAMETER: 11.8 cm

DIAMETER AT BOTTOM OF RIM OR NECK: 10.9 cm

BASE DIAMETER: 6.9 cm

ESTIMATED VOLUME: 0.3 liters

DECORATION: Semi-circular engraved motifs repeated five times around the rim; a white kaolin clay pigment has been rubbed in the engraved lines. The semi-circle motif consist of two semi-circles within a panel defined by upper and lower horizontal engraved lines that encircle the vessel, and within the smaller semi-circle is a small circle and hatched cross element (Figure 68). Each of the semi-circles is divided by hatched hourglass-shaped zones.

TYPE: Ripley Engraved, a Late Caddo Titus phase ceramic type (Suhm and Jelks 1962; Thurmond 1980). The motif on this vessel is not one of the 11 common Ripley Engraved motifs on carinated bowls or compound bowls (Thurmond 1990:Figure 6), though the circle and hatched cross element is used on the scroll and circle and circle and nested triangle motifs.

Figure 68. Ripley Engraved bowl from the Greasy Creek area, Camp County, Texas.

Documentation of Associated and Unassociated Caddo Funerary Objects

SITE NO.: Unknown, but Greasy Creek area (probably 41CP71)

FEATURE: None

VESSEL NO.: 31.6

NON-PLASTICS: grog and bone

VESSEL FORM: small carinated bowl, with direct rim and a rounded, exterior folded lip (Figure 69)

CORE COLOR: A (fired and cooled in an oxidizing or high oxygen environment)

INTERIOR SURFACE COLOR: light yellowish-brown (10YR 6/4)

EXTERIOR SURFACE COLOR: very pale brown (10YR 7/4)

WALL THICKNESS: 4.1 mm at the rim

INTERIOR SURFACE TREATMENT: smoothed on rim

EXTERIOR SURFACE TREATMENT: smoothed on rim

HEIGHT: 4.6 cm

ORIFICE DIAMETER: 11.0 cm

DIAMETER AT BOTTOM OF RIM OR NECK: 10.1 cm

BASE DIAMETER: 4.3 cm

ESTIMATED VOLUME: 0.3 liters

DECORATION: Plain

TYPE: Undetermined plain ware vessel

Figure 69. Undetermined plain carinated bowl from the Greasy Creek area, Camp County, Texas.

Appendix 4

Vessel Recordation Forms for NAGPRA Collections from 41NA113

Documentation of Associated and Unassociated Caddo Funerary Objects

SITE NO.: 41NA113

FEATURE: Burial 1

VESSEL NO.: 113.1

NON-PLASTICS: grog and hematite

VESSEL FORM: bowl with a direct rim and a rounded lip

CORE COLOR: Undetermined

INTERIOR SURFACE COLOR: brown (10YR 4/3)

EXTERIOR SURFACE COLOR: dark brown (10YR 3/3)

WALL THICKNESS: 6.4 mm

INTERIOR SURFACE TREATMENT: burnished

EXTERIOR SURFACE TREATMENT: burnished

HEIGHT: 6.5 cm

ORIFICE DIAMETER: 11.7 cm

DIAMETER AT BOTTOM OF RIM OR NECK: N/A

BASE DIAMETER: 5.4 cm

ESTIMATED VOLUME: 0.4 liters

DECORATION: Sets of fine-line engraved concentric circles (four in each set) repeated four times around the vessel (Figure 70). The concentric circles abut each other around a central circle, suggesting interlocking or hooked arms, a decorative element noted in Taylor Engraved vessels (see Suhm and Jelks 1962: Plates 75m and 76j).

TYPE: Undetermined engraved ware.

Figure 70. Engraved bowl from 41NA113.

Documentation of Associated and Unassociated Caddo Funerary Objects

SITE NO.: 41NA113

FEATURE: Burial 1

VESSEL NO.: 113.2

NON-PLASTICS: None apparent

VESSEL FORM: Bowl with an inverted rim and a rounded lip

CORE COLOR: Undetermined

INTERIOR SURFACE COLOR: black (10YR 2/1)

EXTERIOR SURFACE COLOR: black (10YR 2/1)

WALL THICKNESS: 5.4 mm

INTERIOR SURFACE TREATMENT: smoothed

EXTERIOR SURFACE TREATMENT: burnished

HEIGHT: 4.2 cm

ORIFICE DIAMETER: 7.2 cm

DIAMETER AT BOTTOM OF RIM OR NECK: N/A

BASE DIAMETER: 4.5 cm

ESTIMATED VOLUME: 0.15 liters

DECORATION: Engraved on the upper body of the vessel with two different elements: a, a single row of triangular tick marks pendant from a horizontal line under the lip; and b, sets of interlocking semi-circles (three lines per set), one of which extends to the ticked rim line (Figure 71). A white kaolin clay pigment has been rubbed in the engraved lines, and a red pigment is visible haphazardly across the exterior vessel surface. The lower vessel body has horizontal brushing marks on it.

TYPE: Patton Engraved

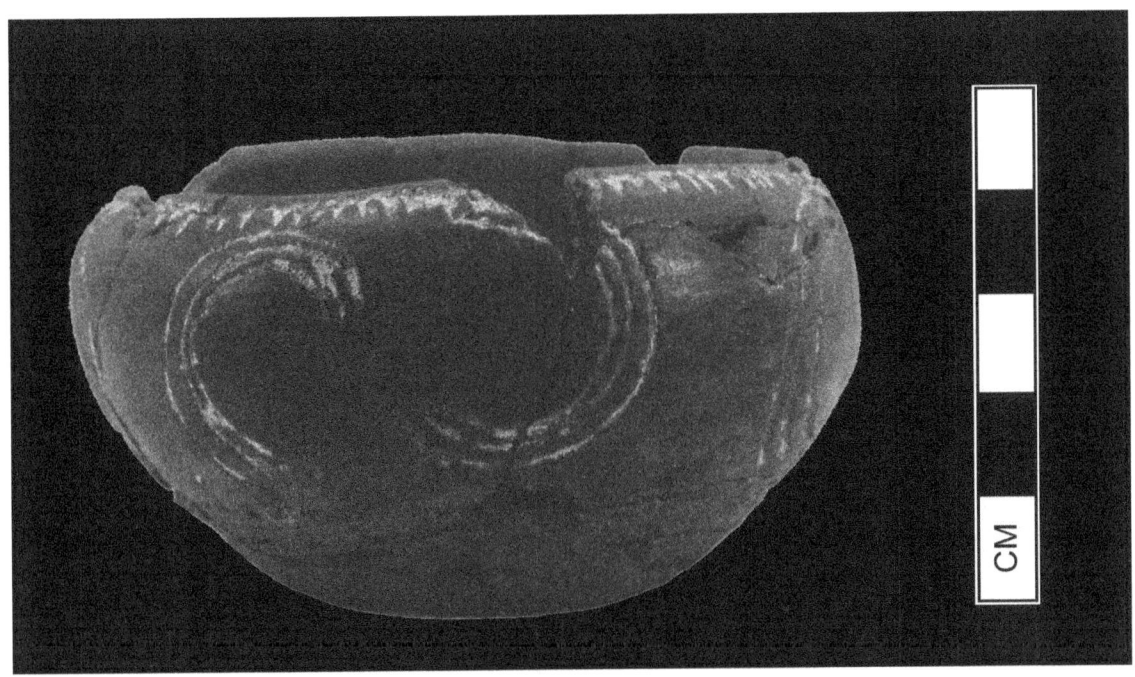

Figure 71. Patton Engraved bowl from 41NA113.

Appendix 5

Vessel Recordation Forms for NAGPRA Collections from 41PN48

Documentation of Associated and Unassociated Caddo Funerary Objects

SITE NO.: 41PN48

FEATURE: Burial 1

VESSEL NO.: 48-1

NON-PLASTICS: grog, bone, and hematite

VESSEL FORM: Bottle with a tapered neck; the rim and lip of the neck has been broken off

CORE COLOR: B (fired and cooled in a reducing environment)

INTERIOR SURFACE COLOR: black (10YR 3/1)

EXTERIOR SURFACE COLOR: black (10YR 3/1)

WALL THICKNESS: 4.8 mm

INTERIOR SURFACE TREATMENT: none

EXTERIOR SURFACE TREATMENT: smoothed

HEIGHT: 5.3 cm+

ORIFICE DIAMETER: 2.6 cm

DIAMETER AT BOTTOM OF RIM OR NECK: 3.1 cm

BASE DIAMETER: Undetermined because of rounded base

ESTIMATED VOLUME: Undetermined

DECORATION: Lightly brushed on the bottle body with opposed brushing marks (Figure 72)

TYPE: Undetermined utility ware vessel.

Figure 72. Brushed bottle from 41PN48.

SITE NO.: 41PN48

FEATURE: Burial 1

VESSEL NO.: 48-2

NON-PLASTICS: grog and hematite; the vessel has a sandy paste

VESSEL FORM: Carinated bowl with an everted rim and a rounded lip (Figure 73)

CORE COLOR: Undetermined

INTERIOR SURFACE COLOR: dark brown (10YR 3/3)

EXTERIOR SURFACE COLOR: very dark brown (10YR 3/2)

WALL THICKNESS: 5.1 mm

INTERIOR SURFACE TREATMENT: burnished

EXTERIOR SURFACE TREATMENT: burnished

HEIGHT: 3.9 cm

ORIFICE DIAMETER: 9.7 cm

DIAMETER AT BOTTOM OF RIM OR NECK: 8.8 cm

BASE DIAMETER: 6.3 cm

ESTIMATED VOLUME: 0.2 liters

DECORATION: Plain

TYPE: Undetermined plain ware

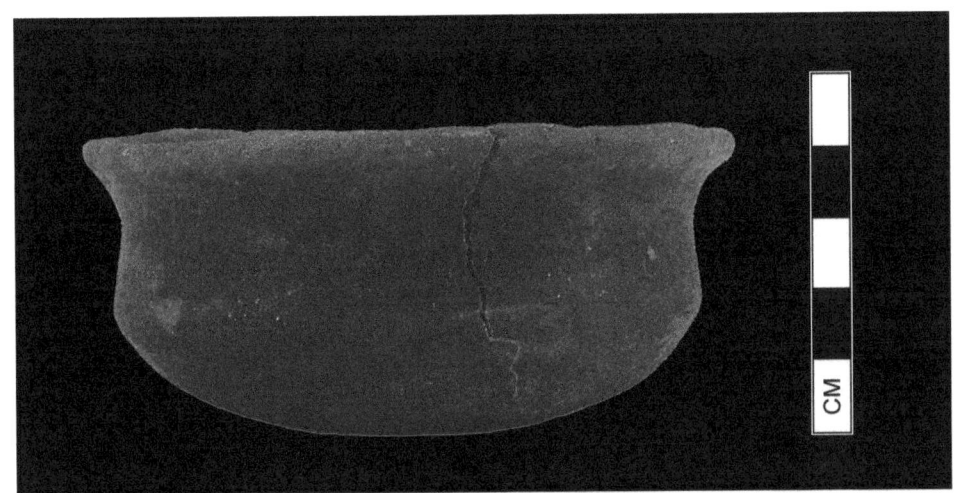

Figure 73. Plain carinated bowl, PN48-2, from 41PN48.

Documentation of Associated and Unassociated Caddo Funerary Objects

SITE NO.: 41PN48

FEATURE: Burial 1

VESSEL NO.: 48-3

NON-PLASTICS: bone, grog, hematite, and charred organic remains

VESSEL FORM: Jar with an everted rim and a rounded lip

CORE COLOR: E (incompletely oxidized during firing)

INTERIOR SURFACE COLOR: dark yellowish-brown (10YR 3/4)

EXTERIOR SURFACE COLOR: dark yellowish-brown (10YR 4/4)

WALL THICKNESS: 5.9 mm

INTERIOR SURFACE TREATMENT: smoothed

EXTERIOR SURFACE TREATMENT: smoothed

HEIGHT: 8.7 cm

ORIFICE DIAMETER: 9.0 cm

DIAMETER AT BOTTOM OF RIM OR NECK: 8.4 cm

BASE DIAMETER: 8.4 cm

ESTIMATED VOLUME: 0.5 liters

DECORATION: The jar rim has horizontal brushing marks, and the body has vertical brushing (Figure 74).

TYPE: Bullard Brushed?

Figure 74. Brushed jar from 41PN48.

Documentation of Associated and Unassociated Caddo Funerary Objects

SITE NO.: 41PN48

FEATURE: Burial 1

VESSEL NO.: 48-4

NON-PLASTICS: bone and hematite

VESSEL FORM: Simple bowl with a direct rim and a rounded lip (Figure 75)

CORE COLOR: Undetermined

INTERIOR SURFACE COLOR: gray (10YR 5/1)

EXTERIOR SURFACE COLOR: dark gray (10YR 4/1)

WALL THICKNESS: 5.7 mm

INTERIOR SURFACE TREATMENT: burnished

EXTERIOR SURFACE TREATMENT: burnished

HEIGHT: 3.0 cm

ORIFICE DIAMETER: Undetermined

DIAMETER AT BOTTOM OF RIM OR NECK: N/A

BASE DIAMETER: Undetermined

ESTIMATED VOLUME: Undetermined, but less than 0.5 liters

DECORATION: Plain

TYPE: Undetermined plain ware vessel

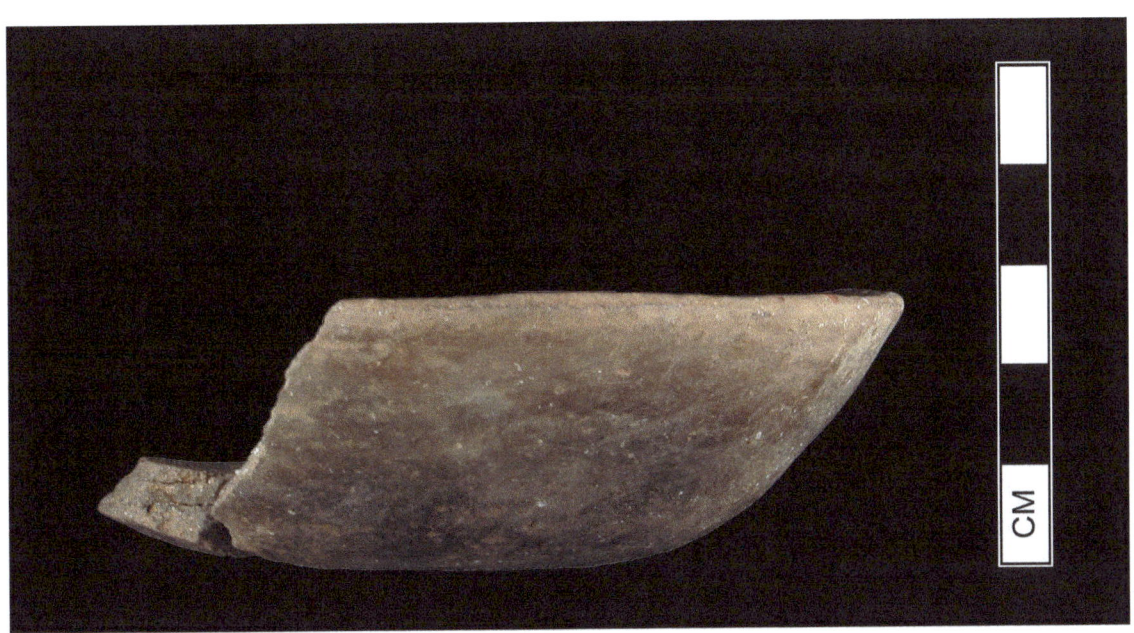

Figure 75. Plain bowl from 41PN48, PN48-4.

Appendix 6

Vessel Recordation Forms for NAGPRA Collections from 41TT135

SITE NO.: 41TT135

FEATURE: 1

VESSEL NO.: 4.1

NON-PLASTICS: bone and hematite

VESSEL FORM: bowl with a direct rim and a rounded lip (Figure 76)

CORE COLOR: F (fired in a reducing environment but cooled in the open air)

INTERIOR SURFACE COLOR: dark grayish-brown (10YR 4/2)

EXTERIOR SURFACE COLOR: grayish-brown (10YR 5/2)

WALL THICKNESS: 5.6 mm

INTERIOR SURFACE TREATMENT: smoothed

EXTERIOR SURFACE TREATMENT: smoothed

HEIGHT: 9.3 cm

ORIFICE DIAMETER: 20.5 cm

DIAMETER AT BOTTOM OF RIM OR NECK: N/A

BASE DIAMETER: 7.9 cm

ESTIMATED VOLUME: 1.1 liters

DECORATION: Plain

TYPE: Undetermined plain ware vessel

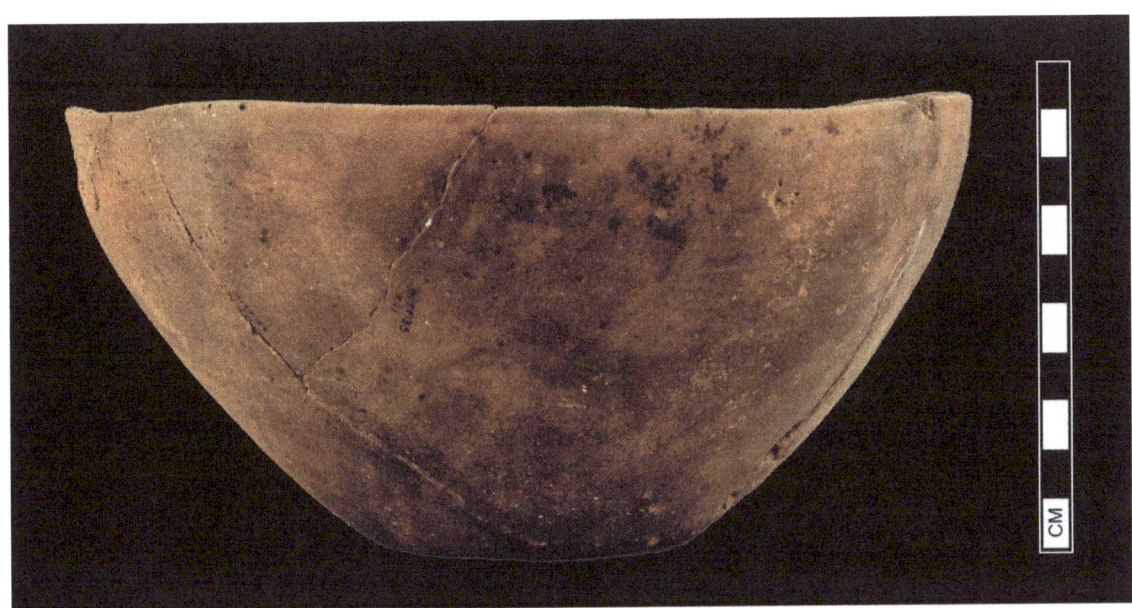

Figure 76. Plain bowl from 41TT135.

Appendix 7
Arrow Points from the Oak Grove Cemetery

Documentation of Associated and Unassociated Caddo Funerary Objects

Subsequent to our documentation of the NAGPRA materials at Stephen F. Austin State University (SFA), 14 of the 15 arrow points reported to have been found within an incised-punctuated vessel at the Oak Grove cemetery (see Corbin 1980; Corbin and Hart 1998; see Figure 9a, this report) were relocated by George Avery at SFA. Pertinent details on the points recorded by Tom Middlebrook are provided below:

Point No.	length (cm)	width (cm)	thickness (cm)	weight (g)	Raw Material	Notes
1	4.77	1.51	0.46	2.07	petrified wood	
2	3.24	1.29	0.35	1.02	petrified wood	
3	2.77	1.32	0.41	1.04	petrified wood	
4	2.62	1.05	0.27	0.64	petrified wood	
5	1.84	1.16	0.28	0.44	petrified wood	
6	1.82	1.55	0.39	0.84	petrified wood	tip broken off
7	2.42	1.20	0.28	0.60	petrified wood	
8	2.22	1.45	0.27	0.62	petrified wood	
9	2.55	1.39	0.29	0.78	petrified wood	
10	2.28	1.21	0.36	0.62	petrified wood	
11	2.41	1.25	0.29	0.56	petrified wood	
12	2.13	1.02	0.33	0.45	petrified wood	
13	2.48	1.12	0.32	0.64	petrified wood	
14	2.20	0.95	0.24	0.47	petrified wood	

All 14 points are made of petrified wood and appear to be of the Perdiz type (Figure 77). Previous excavations at the Washington Square Mound site (41NA49)—of which the Oak Grove cemetery finds are a part—have recovered primarily Perdiz arrow points from various contexts on property owned by the Nacogdoches Independent School District.

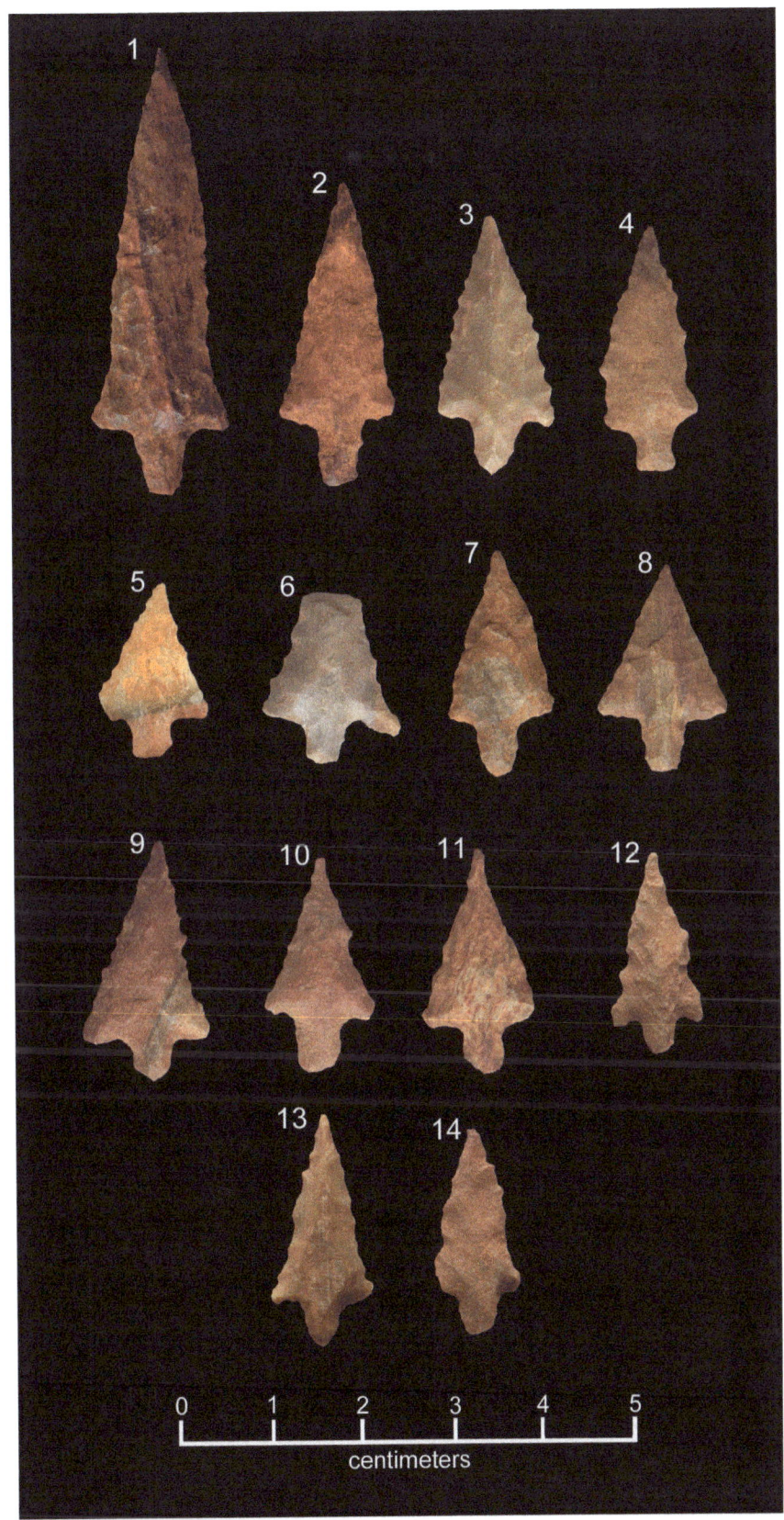

Figure 77. Perdiz arrow points from the vessel found at the Oak Grove cemetery.

Appendix 8

Vessel Recordation Forms for NAGPRA Collections from 41SY83

Documentation of Associated and Unassociated Caddo Funerary Objects

SITE NAME OR SITE NUMBER: 41SY83

VESSEL NO.: No. 1

NON-PLASTICS: grog

VESSEL FORM: Carinated bottle with a straight neck

RIM AND LIP FORM: Direct rim and a rounded lip

CORE COLOR: F (fired in a reducing environment and cooled in the open air)

INTERIOR SURFACE COLOR: reddish-brown (5YR 5/3)

EXTERIOR SURFACE COLOR: reddish-brown (5YR 4/4) with fire clouds on the body and the neck

WALL THICKNESS (RIM, BODY, AND BASE IN MM): 6.3 mm, neck

INTERIOR SURFACE TREATMENT: none

EXTERIOR SURFACE TREATMENT: burnished

HEIGHT (IN CM): 14.5 cm; the neck is 6.0 cm in height

ORIFICE DIAMETER (IN CM): 4.0

DIAMETER AT BOTTOM OF RIM OR NECK (IN CM): 5.0; maximum body diameter is 11.5cm

BASE DIAMETER (IN CM): 6.2 cm

ESTIMATED VOLUME (IN LITERS): 0.36 liters

DECORATION: There are three horizontal engraved lips on the neck, immediately below the lip. The body has both horizontal, diagonal, and near vertical hatched engraved panels, either under the neck or extending along the upper part of the carinated body (Figure 78a-b).

TYPE: unidentified engraved bottle; the hatched vertical and diagonal engraved panels are comparable to other simple engraved bottles from Middle Caddo period contexts in the region.

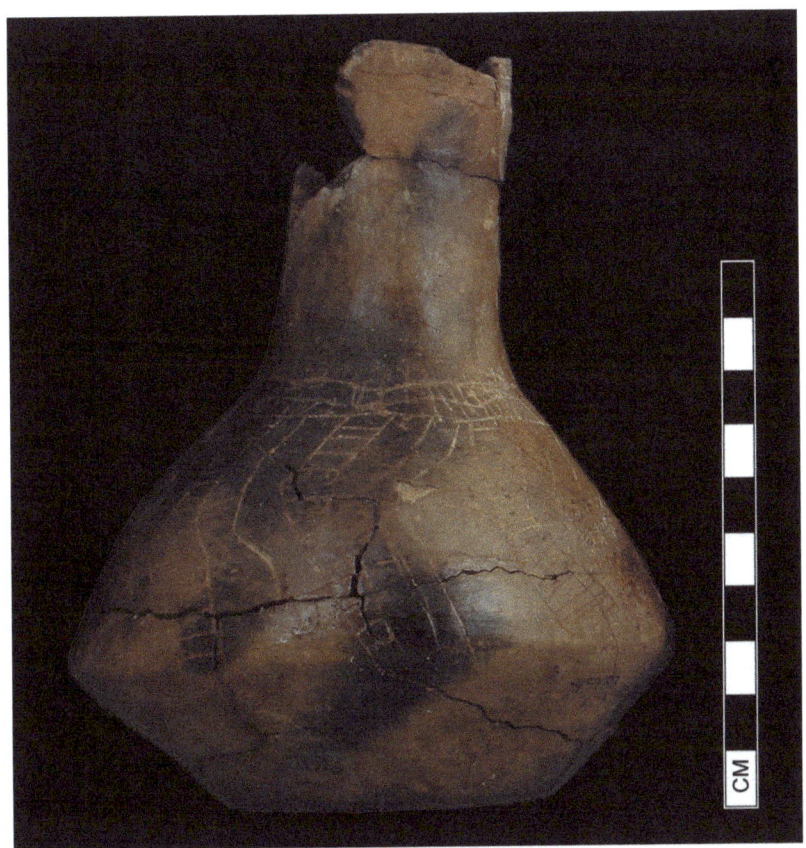

Figure 78a. Engraved bottle from 41SY83, side view.

Figure 78b. Engraved bottle from 41SY83, top view.

Documentation of Associated and Unassociated Caddo Funerary Objects

SITE NAME OR SITE NUMBER: 41SY83

VESSEL NO.: No. 2

NON-PLASTICS: grog

VESSEL FORM: Simple bowl (Figure 79)

RIM AND LIP FORM: Direct rim and rounded lip

CORE COLOR: F (fired in a reducing environment and cooled in the open air)

INTERIOR SURFACE COLOR: brown (7.5YR 5/4)

EXTERIOR SURFACE COLOR: reddish-brown (5YR 4/4)

WALL THICKNESS (RIM, BODY, AND BASE IN MM): 6.0 mm, rim

INTERIOR SURFACE TREATMENT: smoothed

EXTERIOR SURFACE TREATMENT: smoothed

HEIGHT (IN CM): 4.0 cm

ORIFICE DIAMETER (IN CM): 10.0 cm

DIAMETER AT BOTTOM OF RIM OR NECK (IN CM): N/A

BASE DIAMETER (IN CM): 5.5 cm

ESTIMATED VOLUME (IN LITERS): 0.16 liters

DECORATION: Plain

TYPE: Unidentified plain ware vessel

Figure 79. Simple bowl from 41SY83.

SITE NAME OR SITE NUMBER: 41SY83

VESSEL NO.: No. 3

NON-PLASTICS: grog

VESSEL FORM: ladle or dish; oblong-shaped, with possible handle at one end (Figure 80)

RIM AND LIP FORM: Direct rim and a rounded lip

CORE COLOR: F (fired in a reducing environment and cooled in the open air)

INTERIOR SURFACE COLOR: light yellowish-brown (5YR 6/4)

EXTERIOR SURFACE COLOR: reddish-brown (5YR 5/4)

WALL THICKNESS (RIM, BODY, AND BASE IN MM): 6.6 mm, rim; 7.2 mm, body; 8.6 mm, base

INTERIOR SURFACE TREATMENT: smoothed

EXTERIOR SURFACE TREATMENT: smoothed

HEIGHT (IN CM): 5.0 cm

ORIFICE DIAMETER (IN CM): 10.0; 13.5 cm in length from one end to the end of the possible handle

DIAMETER AT BOTTOM OF RIM OR NECK (IN CM): N/A

BASE DIAMETER (IN CM): 7.0 cm

ESTIMATED VOLUME (IN LITERS): 0.20 liters

DECORATION: Plain

TYPE: Unidentified plain ware vessel

List of Authors

Timothy K. Perttula, Archeological & Environmental Consultants, LLC

Mark Walters, Research Fellow, SFA Center for Regional Heritage Research

Bo Nelson, Archeological & Environmental Consultants, LLC

Robert Cast, Tribal Historic Preservation Officer, Caddo Nation

Robert G. Franciscus, University of Iowa

www.ingramcontent.com/pod-product-compliance
Lightning Source LLC
Chambersburg PA
CBHW041102100526
44584CB00050B/4452